Preface

This sketch of Pauline theology has been extracted from a larger work, *The Jerome Biblical Commentary* (edited by Raymond E. Brown, S.S., Roland E. Murphy, O.Carm., and Joseph A. Fitzmyer, S.J.), published by Prentice-Hall. This work is not merely another "introduction" to the Bible but a commentary in the true sense, that is, with comments on the verses. It will also include general articles, such as this sketch of Pauline theology, intended to treat synthetically those subjects that the ordinary analytical comments on the verses cannot adequately cover. This two-part format permits the work to be sufficiently comprehensive and still to suit the practical requirements of ordinary readers. The tone of the commentary is modern, corresponding to the growth of Catholic biblical interpretation.

Like the commentary itself, this sketch is intended for students of the Bible—clerical, religious, and lay. It sets forth in compact form the dominant perspectives of Pauline theology as these are understood today. Detailed explanations of various Pauline passages are not given here because they are treated in the commentaries on the individual letters. Rather, the aim is a synthetic presentation of Pauline thought in its broad outlines.

This sketch has three main parts, a number of subdivisions, and guides to further reading in the principal modern languages at the ends of the various sections. These guides will enable the reader to find his way through the myriad of specialized studies on Pauline topics.

The limited compass of this sketch is due to the place it occupies in the larger work. This necessary brevity has often prevented a more detailed discussion of various points. Cross references to other parts of the *Jerome Biblical Commentary* will supply some of the details omitted here; but these had to be omitted in this separate publication. The abbreviations used here are those that are employed in the commentary.

JAF

iii

Contents

Abbreviations

AbhTANT	Abhandlungen zur Theologie des Alten und Nuen Testaments (Zürich)
Adv. haer.	Irenaeus, Adversus haereses
Adv. Marc.	Tertullian, Adversus Marcionem
AER	American Ecclesiastical Review
AG	W. F. Arndt and F. W. Gingrich, A Greek-English Lexicon of the New Testament (Chicago, 1957)
ALBO	Analecta lovaniensia biblica et orientalia
AnalBib	Analecta biblica (Rome)
Ant.	Josephus, Antiquities of the Jews
app. crit.	critical apparatus (in a Gk NT text)
ASNU	Acta seminarii neotestamentici upsaliensis (Uppsala)
BBB	Bonner biblische Beiträge (Bonn)
Bib	Biblica
BKW	Bible Key Words (ed. J. R. Coates; London)
Bl-Deb-F	F. Blass and A. Debrunner, A Greek Grammar of the New Testament (tr. R. W. Funk; Chicago, 1961)
BWANT	Beiträge zur Wissenschaft von Alten und Neuen Testament (Stuttgart)
CanJT	Canadian Journal of Theology
CBQ	Catholic Biblical Quarterly
CSEL	Corpus scriptorum ecclesiasticorum latinorum (Vienna)
DJD	Discoveries in the Judaean Desert (of Jordan) (Oxford, 1955)
EBib	Études bibliques (Paris)
ETL	Ephemerides theologicae lovanienses
ExpT	Expository Times
Fest.	Festschrift (the siglum for any memorial or commemorative volume despite its language; the name of the person honored follows)
FRLANT	Forschungen zur Religion und Literatur des Alten und Neuen Testaments (Göttingen)
GCS	Griechische christliche Schriftsteller (Berlin)
Greg	Gregorianum
HarvTR	Harvard Theological Review
HE	Eusebius, Historia ecclesiastica

PAULINE THEOLOGY

A Brief Sketch

Joseph A. Fitzmyer, S. J.
Woodstock College

PRENTICE-HALL, INC.   *Englewood Cliffs, New Jersey*

Imprimi potest
  Edward J. Sponga, S.J.
  Provincial of the Maryland Province

Nihil obstat
  Raymond E. Brown, S.S.
  Censor Deputatus

Imprimatur
  ✠ Lawrence Cardinal Shehan
  Archbishop of Baltimore
November 8, 1966

Current printing (last digit):

17   16   15   14

Library of Congress Catalog Card No.: 67–19295
Printed in the United States of America

PRENTICE-HALL INTERNATIONAL, INC., *London*
PRENTICE-HALL OF AUSTRALIA, PTY. LTD., *Sydney*
PRENTICE-HALL OF CANADA, LTD., *Toronto*
PRENTICE-HALL OF INDIA PRIVATE LTD., *New Delhi*
PRENTICE-HALL OF JAPAN, INC., *Tokyo*

HTS	Harvard Theological Studies (Cambridge, Mass.)
IDB	Interpreter's Dictionary of the Bible (ed. G. A. Buttrick; 4 vols.; Nashville, 1963)
Interpr	Interpretation
IPLAP	B. M. Metzger, Index to Periodical Literature on the Apostle Paul (NTTS 1; Leiden, 1960)
ITNT	A. Richardson, Introduction to the Theology of the New Testament (London, 1958)
JBL	Journal of Biblical Literature
JTS	Journal of Theological Studies
LAE	A. Deissmann, Light from the Ancient East (London, 1927)
LD	Lectio divina (Paris)
LumVi	Lumière et Vie (St. Alban-Leysse)
LXX	Septuagint (Gk translation of the OT)
Midr. Eccl.	Midrash on Ecclesiastes
NEB	New English Bible (Oxford and Cambridge, 1961)
NRT	Nouvelle revue théologique
NT	New Testament
NTAbh	Neutestamentliche Abhandlungen (Münster)
NTS	New Testament Studies
OT	Old Testament
Q	Qumran
QL	Qumran Literature
RB	Revue biblique
RBiblt	Rivista biblica italiana
R-F, Int	A. Robert and A. Feuillet, Introduction to the New Testament (tr. P. W. Skehan, et al.; N.Y., 1965)
RHPR	Revue d'histoire et de philosophie religieuses
RSPT	Revue des sciences philosophiques et theologiques (Paris)
SBT	Studies in Biblical Theology (London and Naperville, Ill.)
ScotJT	Scottish Journal of Theology
SP	Sacra pagina (2 vols.; Gembloux, 1954)
StANT	Studien z. Alten u. Neuen Testament (Munich)
Tg. Ct	Targum on Canticles
Tg. Is	Targum on Isaiah
TGl	Theologie und Glaube
ThDNT	G. Kittel (ed.) Theological Dictionary of the New Testament (Grand Rapids, 1964–; = Engl. version of ThWNT)
ThWNT	G. Kittel (ed.), Theologisches Wörterbuch zum Neuen Testament (8 vols.; Stuttgart, 1933–)
TLZ	Theologische Literaturzeitung
TNT	R. Bultmann, The Theology of the New Testament (2 vols.; N.Y., 1954)

TQ	*Theologische Quartalschrift*
TRu	*Theologische Rundschau*
TS	*Theological Studies*
TTod	*Theology Today*
VD	*Verbum domini*
VDBS	F. Vigouroux, *Dictionnaire de la Bible, Supplément* (7 vols.; Paris, 1928–)
VerbC	*Verbum caro*
Vg	Vulgate
VP	*Vivre et penser* (= RB 1941–44)
WMzANT	Wissenschaftliche Monographien zum Alten und Neuen Testament
ZNW	*Zeitschrift für die neutestamentliche Wissenschaft*
ZThK	*Zeitschrift für Theologie und Kirche*

Apocryphal Books

Apoc. Mos.	*Apocalypse of Moses*
Enoch	Ethiopic *Enoch* (= First Enoch)
2 Enoch	Slavonic *Enoch* (= *Book of the Secrets of Enoch*)
2 Esdras	4 Esdras in the Vg (= *Apocalypse of Ezra* or *4 Ezra*)
Jub	*Jubilees*

Miscellaneous Abbreviations

b	Babylonian Talmud (followed by name of specific tractate)
j	Jerusalem Talmud (followed by name of specific tractate)
jMeg.	Jerusalem Talmud, tractate *Megilloth*
1QS	Manual of Discipline from Qumran Cave 1
1QH	Hymns of Thanksgiving from Qumran Cave 1
1QM	War Scroll from Qumran Cave 1
1QSa	Rule of the Congregation from Qumran Cave 1 (= 1Q28 in DJD 1)
1QapGn	*Genesis Apocryphon* from Qumran Cave 1
4QFlor	Florilegium from Qumran Cave 4

Aims, Limits, Problems

A sketch of Pauline theology must take into account the character of the Apostle's writings, which do not offer a systematic presentation of his thought. Most of what Paul wrote was composed *ad hoc* —for the handling of concrete situations by letter. In his letters Paul developed certain doctrinal topics and exhorted his churches to the practice of a more intense Christian life. Almost every extant letter exemplifies this twofold purpose. This dual purpose explains how he could mingle in them elements of revelation, fragments of the primitive kerygma, teachings of Christ, interpretations of the OT, a personal understanding of the Christ-event, and even his own private opinions. Therefore, any attempt to formulate Pauline "theology" must also try to reckon with the varied nuances of the Apostle's thought and expression.

Moreover, a presentation of "Pauline theology" is an admission that Paul's view of the Christian experience is but one among several theologies in the NT. It is imperative to respect Paul's theology and not to confuse it with John's, Luke's, or any other's. It must be studied in and for itself. This admonition is not meant to imply that a NT theology is impossible or that contradictions are to be expected between Paul and another NT writer. The NT books bear witness to a faith in one Lord, one baptism, one God and Father of all (Eph 4:5–6), and a theology explaining that one faith is not an impossibility. But its presentation will be the richer if the nuances of the individual NT writers are respected.

A sketch of Pauline theology is a systematization of the Apostle's thought in a form in which he himself did not present it. If such a systematization forces his thought into categories foreign to it, or attempts merely to line up *dicta probantia* for a theological system born of another inspiration, it has little value. The effort to synthesize Paul's thought must respect his categories as far as possible, with due allowance for the unequal degree of his affirmations and

1

the diversity of the contexts in which he formulated it. The guiding principle of such a sketch, therefore, cannot be an extrinsic one, be it Aristotelian, Thomistic, Hegelian, or Heideggerian.

Though the primary aim of this sketch is a descriptive presentation of Paul's view of Christian faith, it also intends to be a normative theological presentation. It aims above all at determining what Paul meant when he wrote to the Christians whom he immediately addressed, but it also aims at ascertaining what his theology means for Christians of today. This sketch is not merely a study of Paul's thought as a historian of religion might pursue it (be he agnostic or believer); it does not attempt merely to determine what Paul taught, what influenced him, or how his teachings fit into the general history of Jewish, Hellenistic, or Christian ideas. Paul's theology is an exposition of the inspired biblical heritage of Christians, and the Word of God proposed in his exposé still has an existential meaning for the faith of men of today. In this way, Paul's theology is a *part* of normative biblical theology, just as biblical theology itself is only a part of normative theology as such. There are two poles in biblical theology, one descriptive, the other normative.

It is important to emphasize that the "meaning for the faith of men of today" cannot be something completely other than the meaning intended by Paul for his contemporaries. Any attempt to understand him that fails to recognize a radical homogeneity between his meaning "now" and "then" fails to bring *his* inspired message to men of today. A valid sketch of Pauline theology must, therefore, ascertain first of all what Paul meant and in this sense must be a descriptive presentation. The means to achieve this are not the logic or the metaphysics of some system of philosophy foreign to him, however legitimate and fruitful this mode of interpretation might be for other purposes. The means are rather those of philological, historical, and literary research, joined to an empathy of Christian faith. In other words, the one who sketches Paul's theology in a descriptive presentation shares with Paul the same faith and seeks through it to determine his meaning for today. Although the biblical theologian, in attempting to discover what Paul meant, employs the same tools of interpretation that the historian of religion—or, for that matter, the interpreter of any ancient document—uses, he differs in that he is convinced that through Paul "the one Lord . . . the one God and Father of us all" (Eph 4:5–6) is communicating an inspired message to him and to the men of his time. His fundamental presupposition is the inspired character of the Pauline corpus, a matter of *faith*. He seeks to sketch Paul's exposé and understanding of Christian faith in a way that is meaningful and relevant for Christians of a later age.

This empathy of Christian faith is sometimes expressed in terms of the "analogy of faith," a phrase derived ultimately from Paul himself (Rom 12:6). It cannot be used to insist that the totality of Christian faith has to be found in Paul or even that his thought *must* be interpreted according to the sense of later dogmatic progress, with all its precisions and specific nuances. If a seminal notion formulated by Paul has in time undergone further dogmatic development because of a polemical situation or a conciliar decision in the Church, then that seminal notion must be recognized as such. It may be that the seminal notion is expressed by Paul in a vague, "open" fashion; thus formulated, it could conceivably have developed in one way or another, as far as one can judge today with philological criteria. But the further dogmatic development has removed that *openness* of formulation, so far as Christian tradition is concerned. Yet this does not mean that the historian of dogma or the dogmatic theologian can insist that this later development is the precise meaning of the text of Paul. Neither kind of scholar enjoys a charism whereby he can read more in an "open" Pauline text than can the exegete or the biblical theologian. To understand the "analogy of faith" in such a way as to read back into Paul a later meaning would be false to him and to the inspired autonomy of his conception and formulation. Rather, that analogy must be understood in terms of the total Pauline, biblical faith. Obviously, the biblical theologian is not content merely with the interpretation of individual passages in their immediate context (i.e., with exegesis). He seeks the expression of the total Pauline message, which transcends the contextual situation and embraces also the relational meaning of Pauline utterances.

Though normative biblical theology is only a part of the larger complex of Christian theology, it does enjoy its own autonomy of formulation and conception. True, it is only inceptive. But it is also privileged, for it attempts to formulate systematically what the witnesses of the early Christian tradition were inspired to set down in their own way. It deals immediately and exclusively with the form of Christian tradition that alone enjoys the distinctive divine charism of inspiration that guarantees it. It goes without saying that for a Christian the guidance of the Spirit has guarded the authentic dogmatic developments of later times from a contradiction of the seminal formulations and conceptions. But such protection does not mean that the full flower is already present in the seed. Hence the need to respect Pauline theology for what it is.

This sketch of Pauline theology reckons with ten letters in the Pauline corpus. The theology of Heb is a problem apart and should not be treated with Paul's theology. Likewise, the material in Acts bearing on Paul's teaching can be used only for comparative purposes because of the Lucan cast given to it. The "Pastoral Letters" create another problem because of the present debate about their authenticity. We have followed the lead of several modern Catholic writers in omitting data from them in such a sketch, except for the purpose of comparison at certain points (references to them are bracketed). For the rest, we divide Paul's letters into three chronological groups: *Early Letters:* 1–2 Thes (AD 50–51); *Great Letters:* Gal, Phil, 1–2 Cor, Rom (AD 54–58); *Captivity Letters:* Phlm, Col, Eph (AD 61–63).

We admit a certain development in Paul's theology from one group of letters to another—a development, however, that is influenced by many factors. Perhaps the development is best seen in terms of emphasis, but one can also distinguish a certain growth in his understanding of the Christ-event as one moves from group to group. For instance, in the Early Letters there is only an extrinsic connection between the glorious resurrection of the Christian and Christ's resurrection (1 Thes 4:14: Through Jesus God will lead those who have died with him). It is set forth in an apocalyptic description of the *eschaton,* reflecting the primitive eschatology of the early Church. In the Great Letters the emphasis shifts to an intimate connection between the passion, death, and resurrection of Christ and man's salvation. Through the passion, death, and resurrection Christ has become a "power" (*dynamis*) producing a new life in the Christian believer, which eventually ensures his resurrection and life "with Christ." There is also his view of this new life as the "justification" of man, a juridical aspect that emerges from the Judaizing controversy in the early Church. There is, further, the shift in Paul's views of death and the destiny of the Christian (2 Cor 5:16–21).

Finally, in the Captivity Letters Paul arrives at a fuller view of the Risen Christ as the one who gives man's history a fullness and cosmic dimension that it was not suspected to have earlier. To this cosmic view of Christ not only the universe but the Church itself is related.

(Allo, E.-B., "L'évolution de l'Évangile de Paul," *VP* 1 [1941] 48–77, 165–93. Ebeling, G., "The Meaning of 'Biblical Theology,'" *JTS* 6 [1955] 210–25. Lester-Garland, L. V., "The Sequence of Thought in the Pauline Epistles," *Theology* 33 [1936] 228–38. Lowe, J., "An Examination of Attempts to Detect Developments in St. Paul's Theology," *JTS* 42 [1941] 129–42. Richardson, A., "Historical Theology and Biblical Theology," *CanJT* 1 [1955] 157–67. Schnackenburg, R., *Neutestamentliche Theologie,* 11–14; *New Testament Theology Today* [N.Y., 1962] 15–23. Spicq, C., "L'avènement de la théologie biblique," *RSPT* 35 [1951] 561–74. Stendahl, K., "Biblical Theology, Contemporary," *IDB* 1. 418–32.)

Background

Five factors that influenced Paul's theology can be considered; not all of them are of equal importance.

(I) **Pharisaic, Rabbinical Background.** The polemical passages in which Paul so resolutely rejects the Law should not be allowed to obscure the fact that even the Christian Paul looked back with pride on his life as a Jew of the Pharisaic tradition, trained in Jerusalem (Phil 3:5–6; Gal 1:14; 2 Cor 11:22). This strong Jewish background accounts for the fact that he thinks and expresses himself in OT categories and images. It also accounts for his abundant use of the OT (which he cites some 90 times explicitly). Though his use of the OT is often similar to that of the Qumran writings and of early rabbinical compositions, he usually quotes it according to the LXX. At times, like the rabbis, he accommodates or gives new meaning to OT passages (Hab 2:4 in Rom 1:17 or Gal 3:11; Gn 12:7 in Gal 3:16; Ex 34:34 in 2 Cor 3:17) or allegorizes them (Gn 16:15; 17:16 in Gal 4:21ff.) or wrests them from their original context (Dt 25:4 in 1 Cor 9:9) or utterly disregards their literal meaning (Ps 68:19 in Eph 4:8). Paul's use of the OT does not conform to our modern ideas of quoting Scripture. His mode of interpreting it may seem to be cavalier, but it does agree with the contemporary Jewish way of interpreting the OT and must be accepted as such. That he was inspired by the Spirit to interpret it in this fashion does not mean that his interpretation always reveals a hidden, deeper (literal) sense otherwise unsuspected. His rabbinical training permitted him to accommodate the text at times too. Again, it is his Jewish background that makes him quote the OT to stress the unity of God's action in both dispensations, for he often cites the OT as announcing the Christian gospel (Rom 1:2) or as preparing for Christ (Gal 3:24). Even if he contrasts the "letter [or the Law] and the Spirit" (Rom 2:29, 27; 7:6–7; 2 Cor 3:6–7), the OT is still for him a means through which God speaks to men (1 Cor 9:10; 2

6

Cor 6:16, 17; cf. Rom 4:23). Most of his theology (in the narrow sense, teaching about God) and his anthropology (teaching about man) clearly reveals his Jewish background.

(Bonsirven, J., *Exégèse rabbinique et exégèse paulinienne* [Paris, 1939]. Davies, W. D., *Paul and Rabbinic Judaism* [2nd ed.; London, 1958]. Ellis, E. E., *Paul's Use of the OT* [Edinburgh, 1957]. Fitzmyer, J. A., "The Use of Explicit OT Quotations in Qumran Literature and in the NT," *NTS* 7 [1960–61] 297–333. Marmorstein, A., "Paulus und die Rabbinen," *ZNW* 30 [1931] 271–85. Michel, O., *Paulus und seine Bibel* [Gütersloh, 1929]. Thackeray, H. S. J., *The Relation of St. Paul to Contemporary Jewish Thought* [London, 1900]. Windisch, H., *Paulus und das Judentum* [Stuttgart, 1935].)

(II) **Hellenism.** If the thesis of W. C. van Unnik is accepted, then Paul, though born in Tarsus, was brought up in Jerusalem and there educated at the feet of Gamaliel in the traditions of the Fathers (see Acts 22:3 [NEB]; cf. 26:4–5; 23:6; Phil 3:5; *Tarsus or Jerusalem: The City of Paul's Youth* [London, 1962]). This reconstruction of Paul's youth would entail a reassessment of the influence of Hellenistic culture on his theology. It would mean that Aramaic was the language in which he was brought up and that Greek was learned as a second tongue. This would at least explain why his Greek is not the literary Koine and why it manifests Aramaisms at times (see W. C. van Unnik, *Vox theologica* 14 [1943] 117–26).

However, there is evidence of the influence of the Gk world in his style and also in his use of the LXX. Paul knew Greek and had some sort of Gk training. If he did not become a professional *rhetor*, his mode of expression reveals, at least at times, the influence of Gk rhetoric. There are traces in Paul of the Cynic-Stoic mode of argumentation called *diatribē*, a discourse conducted in a familiar, conversational style, which developed often by lively argument with a fictitious opponent; its sentence structure is brief, and questions are interjected; antitheses and parallel phrases often punctuate the development. Good examples are found in Rom 2:1–20 and 1 Cor 9. Many of Paul's literary antitheses have also been traced to Gk influence (see J. Nélis, *NRT* 70 [1948] 360–87). It was once fashionable to trace to Paul's Hellenistic background such terms as "Lord," "Son of God," "body," "flesh and spirit," and "mystery" and to ascribe to Hellenistic Gnosticism his use of "Adam" and "Man," the redeemer myth, pre-existence, instrumentality in creation, and so forth. However, many of these notions have been shown in recent times to have been at home in 1st-cent. Palestinian Judaism, which was not entirely isolated from the Hellenistic world. The whole question of the influence of Gk culture on Paul's thought and theology needs reassessment today. Paul lived for roughly ten years in a Hellenistic atmosphere, after his conversion and before his first mission, in such cultural centers as Damascus, Tarsus, and Antioch. This Gk atmosphere cannot be lightly dismissed. Its influence is seen in the figures and illustrations he uses. Whereas Jesus' illustrations reflect the agrarian life of Galilee, Paul frequently uses images that are derived from a city-culture, especially a Hellenistic one. He uses Gk political terminology (Phil 1:27; 3:20; Eph 2:19); alludes to Gk games (Phil 2:16; 3:14; 1 Cor 9:24–27; 2 Cor 4:8–9); employs Gk commercial terms (Phlm 18; Col 2:14), Gk legal terminology (Gal 3:15; 4:1–2; Rom 7:1–3); and refers to Hellenistic slave trade (1 Cor 7:22; Rom 7:14) and the Hellenistic celebration in honor of the emperor (1 Thes 2:19). (See F. W. Beare, *CanJT* 5 [1959] 84–85.)

(Bultmann, R., "Paulus und der Hellenismus," *TLZ* 72 [1947] 77–80. Jeremias, J., "The Key to Pauline Theology," *ExpT* 76 [1964–65] 27–30. Klausner, J., *From Jesus to Paul* [London, 1946] 450–66. Knox, W. L., *St. Paul and the Church of the Gentiles* [Cambridge, 1939]; *Some Hellenistic Elements in Primitive Christianity* [London, 1944]. Pohlenz, M., "Paulus und die Stoa," *ZNW* 42 [1949] 69–104. Rigaux, B., *Saint Paul et ses lettres*, 35–43.)

(III) The Revelation to Paul.   Paul's theology was influenced most of all by his experience on the road to Damascus and by faith in the Risen Christ as the Son of God, which developed from his experience. New Testament scholars are today less prone than those of former generations to look on that experience as a "conversion" to be psychologically explained in terms of Paul's Jewish background or in terms of Rom 7 (understood as a biographical account). Paul himself speaks of that experience as a revelation of the Son accorded him by the Father (Gal 1:16). In it he "saw Jesus the Lord" (1 Cor 9:1; cf. 1 Cor 15:8; 2 Cor 4:6; Acts 9:5). That revelation of the crucified "Lord of glory" (1 Cor 2:8) was the event that not only turned Paul the Pharisee into an apostle but also made him the first Christian theologian. The only difference between that experience, in which Jesus appeared to him (1 Cor 15:8), and the experience of the official witnesses of the resurrection (Acts 1:22) was that his vision was post-pentecostal. It put him on an equal footing with the Twelve who had seen the *Kyrios*. He later spoke of that experience as one in which he had been "seized" by Christ Jesus (Phil 3:12) and in which a "necessity" had been laid on him to preach the gospel (1 Cor 9:15–18). He compared that experience to God's creation of light: "For it is the God who said, 'Let light shine out of darkness,' who has shone in our hearts to give the light of the knowledge of the glory of God in the face of Christ" (2 Cor 4:6). The compulsion of divine grace pressed him into the service of Christ; he could not kick against the pricks of such a goad (Acts 26:14). His response was one of vivid faith, in which he confessed with the early Church that "Jesus is the Lord" (1 Cor 12:12; cf. Rom 10:9; Phil 2:11). But that experience illumined in a creative act Paul's mind and gave him an extraordinary insight into what he later called "the mystery of Christ" (Eph 3:4).

That "revelation" (Gal 1:16) impressed Paul, *first* of all, with the unity of divine action for the salvation of all men, which is manifest in both the Old and New Dispensations. As a result of that encounter with the Risen Christ, Paul did not become a Marcionite, rejecting the OT. The Father who revealed his Son to Paul was the same God whom Paul the Pharisee had always served. He was the creator, the lord of history, the God who continually saved his people Israel, and who proved to be a faithful lord of the covenant despite Israel's infidelities. Probably because he had been a Pharisee preoccupied with the minutiae of the Law, Paul never manifested a profound understanding of that "covenant." And yet his experience on the road to Damascus did not alter his fundamental commitment to the "one God." Indeed, his theology (in the narrow sense of the word), his cosmology, and his anthropology reveal him still to be a Jew in his basic outlook.

Second, that vision taught him the soteriological value of the death and resurrection of Jesus the Messiah. If his basic theology did not change, his Christology did. As a Jew, Paul had shared the messianic expectations of his time; he looked forward to the coming of a messiah (of some sort). But the vision of Jesus taught him that God's Anointed One had already come, that he was "Jesus who was handed over for our offenses and raised up for our justification" (Rom 4:25). Before his experience on the road to Damascus, Paul certainly knew that Jesus of Nazareth had been crucified, had been "hung on a tree," and hence had been "cursed" in the sense of Dt 21:23. This was undoubtedly one of the reasons why he as a Pharisee could not accept Jesus as the Messiah. He was for Paul "a stumbling block" (1 Cor 1:23), one "cursed" by the very Law which he so zealously observed (Gal 3:13; cf. 1:14; Phil 3:5–6). But the revelation near Damascus impressed him emphatically with the soteriological and vicarious value of the death of Jesus of Nazareth in a way that he never suspected before. With a logic that only a rabbi could appreciate, Paul saw Christ Jesus taking upon himself the Law's curse and transforming it into its opposite, so that he became the means of freeing men from its malediction. The cross, which had been the stumbling block to the Jews, became for him the "power and wisdom of God" (1 Cor 1:18–25). Henceforth, he would understand the crucified "Lord of glory" as his exalted Messiah.

Third, that revelation impressed Paul with a new vision of salvation history. Before the encounter with Jesus the Lord, Paul saw man's history divided into three great phases: (1) from Adam to Moses (the period without the Law); (2) from Moses to the Messiah (the period of the Law); (3) the Messianic age (the period when the Messiah would legislate anew). But the experience on the road to Damascus taught him that the Messianic age had already begun. This introduced a new perspective into his view of salvation history. The *eschaton*, so avidly awaited before, had already begun— although a definitive stage was still to be realized (hopefully not too far in the future). The Messiah had not yet come in glory. Paul realized then that he (with all Christians) found himself in a double situation: one in which he looked back to the death and resurrection of Jesus as the inauguration of the new age, and another in which he still looked forward to his coming in glory, his parousia.

Far more than his Pharisaic background, therefore, or even his Hellenistic cultural roots, that revelation of Jesus gave Paul an ineffable insight into "the mystery of Christ." It enabled him to fashion his "gospel," to preach the fundamental good news in a form that was distinctively his own.

However, Paul did not immediately understand all the implications of the vision accorded to him. It provided only a basic insight, which was to color all that he was to learn about Jesus and his mission among men, not only from the early Church's tradition, but also from his own apostolic experience in preaching "Christ crucified" (Gal 3:1).

(Menoud, P.-H., "Revelation and Tradition: The Influence of Paul's Conversion on His Theology," *Interpr* 7 [1953] 131–41; also *VerbC* 7 [1953] 2–10. Munck, J., "The Call," *Paul and the Salvation of Mankind* [London, 1959] 11–35. Pfaff, E., *Die Bekehrung des h. Paulus* [Rome, 1942]. Rigaux, B., *Saint Paul et ses lettres*, 63–97. Wood, H. G., "The Conversion of St. Paul," *NTS* 1 [1955–56] 276–82.)

(IV) Paul and Early Tradition. If the main inspiration of Paul's theology was the revelation granted to him on the road to Damascus, that event was not the only source of his knowledge about Christ and the Christian movement. He was not the founder of that movement, but joined it after its missionary efforts had already begun. It is a priori likely, then, that Paul inherited from the pioneer tradition of the Church at least some ideas about Christ. At first, this observation might seem to contradict what he himself says in Gal about the origin of his gospel, that he was not taught it and that it came to him rather through a revelation of Jesus Christ (1:11, 15–17; 2:6). Yet here especially we must be sensitive to the nuances of Paul's expression and affirmation, realizing that the passages in Gal were written in the heat of controversy. Paul had been under attack, accused of not being a real apostle and of preaching only a watered-down version of the gospel because of his attitude toward the Law. When he wrote Gal, Paul was at pains, therefore, to emphasize his divine, direct, and undelegated apostolic commission and the heavenly origin of his gospel.

Yet this emphasis must not be allowed to obscure what is found elsewhere in his letters. For there are, in fact, clear indications of his dependence on the apostolic tradition of the early Church—on its kerygma, its liturgy, its hymns, its confessional formulas, its theological terminology, and its paraenesis. Fragments of the primitive kerygma are found in Paul's letters (1 Thes 1:10; Gal 1:3–4; 1 Cor 15:2–7; Rom 1:2–4; 2:16; 8:34; 10:8–9). He has incorporated elements of its liturgy, e.g., the Eucharistic formula (of Antiochene origin? 1 Cor 11:23–25); prayers like "Amen" (1 Thes 3:13; Gal 6:18; cf. 1 Cor 14:16; 2 Cor 1:20), "Maranatha" (1 Cor 16:22), "Abba, Father" (Gal 4:6; Rom 8:15); doxologies (Gal 1:5; Phil 4:20; Rom 11:36; 16:27?; Eph 3:21); and hymns (Phil 2:6–11; Col 1:15–20; Eph 5:14; [cf. 1 Tm 3:16]). His confessional formulas, too, undoubtedly echo early Church usage: "Jesus is the Lord" (1 Cor 12:13; Rom 10:9), "Jesus is the Christ" (1 Cor 3:11). He inherited as well a number of theological terms, e.g., the title *Kyrios*, "Son of God"; the word "apostle"; the expression *baptizō eis*, "church of God," etc. Finally, certain hortatory sections of his letters suggest by the terminology employed that Paul is incorporating paraenetic or catechetical material drawn from common usage (1 Thes 4:1–12; 1 Cor 6:9–10; Gal 5:19–21; Eph 5:5–21).

Moreover, there are times when Paul explicitly calls attention to the fact that he is "handing down" (*paradidōmi*) what he has "received" (*paralambanō*). (See 1 Cor 11:2, 23; 15:1, 3; cf. 1 Thes 2:13; 2 Thes 2:15; 3:6; Gal 1:9, 12; Phil 4:9; Rom 6:17.) He uses the technical vocabulary of tradition, paralleled in the rabbinical schools (*māsar lᵉ*, "pass on to"; *qibbēl min*, "receive from"). He appeals further to the customs of the churches (1 Cor 11:16) and recommends fidelity to tradition (1 Cor 11:2; 15:2; 2 Thes 2:15). It has been stated by O. Cullmann (*RHPR* 30 [1950] 12–13) that it is surprising to see Paul applying such discredited notions to the normative moral and doctrinal precepts of the primitive community, when one recalls how radically Jesus rejected precisely the *paradosis* of the Jews (cf. Mk 7:3ff.; Mt 15:2). Obviously, there was something here that Paul did not feel that he could dispense with.

Another aspect of Paul's dependence on early Church tradition is seen in his acquaintance with what Jesus did and taught. Paul gives no evidence of having known Jesus personally in his earthly ministry (not even 2 Cor 5:16 necessarily implies that he did). Nor should it be imagined that Paul was granted a cinematic view of that ministry at his conversion. It is remarkable how little he knew of Jesus the Galilean rabbi or even of what is recorded in the Gospels about him. One reason for this is the early date of Paul's letters— almost all of them were written before the Gospels took the form we know. But an even more important reason is the emphasis that Paul, not having been an eyewitness, puts on the salvific effects of the passion, death, and resurrection of Jesus, which transcend the mere historical data. His interest lies in these climactic events of Jesus' life rather than in minutiae about Jesus' manner of life, his ministry, his personality, or even his message. True, he may allude to, or quote a saying of, Jesus occasionally (1 Thes 4:2,15; 1 Cor

7:10 [cf. 25]; 9:14; 13:2; Rom 12:14; 13:9; 16:19; cf. D. M. Stanley, *CBQ* 23 [1961] 26–39; W. D. Davies, *Paul and Rabbinic Judaism,* 136–41), and such quotations reveal that sayings of Jesus were already being handed on in addition to the kerygma. Yet these sayings are often referred to by Paul as sayings of "the Lord" (*Kyrios*), a title that immediately reveals the transcendent aspect under which Paul saw them. He is not interested in the historical Jesus as a teacher, a prophet, or as the chronological source and the first link in the chain of such transmission. Rather, Paul is interested in the exalted Lord who is the real agent of all the tradition developing in the bosom of the apostolic church. This is why he identifies with the *Kyrios* what he has in reality derived from the early community. The *Kyrios* himself is at work in that transmission and as such is the "end of the Law" and the replacement of the *paradosis* of the Jews. Indeed, the *Kyrios* himself is even said to be received by the *paradosis* of the early Church (Col 2:6).

Paul alludes to remarkably few details of the life of Christ: Jesus was born of a woman under the Law (Gal 4:4), was betrayed (1 Cor 11:23), instituted the Eucharist (1 Cor 11:23), was crucified (Gal 2:20; 3:1; Phil 2:5; 1 Cor 2:2, 8), died (1 Cor 15:3), was buried (1 Cor 15:4), was raised from the dead (1 Cor 15:5), and ascended to heaven (Eph 4:9). (1 Tm 6:13 alludes to his testimony before Pilate.) Yet even these few events are not narrated for their own sake or in the manner of the Evangelists; they are, instead, recorded in contexts of a peculiarly theological or kerygmatic character. Possibly, Paul learned this outline of Jesus' last days from the early Church, but probably some of the details were already known to him before his conversion.

Such features as these in Paul's letters suggest that he did derive information from the traditions of the early churches (Jerusalem, Damascus, Antioch). Even his visit to Jerusalem, when he spent 15 days with Cephas (Gal 1:18), would support this. But such information was always transformed by Paul's personal vision and insight.

(Baird, W., "What Is the Kerygma?" *JBL* 76 [1957] 181–91. Cullmann, O., "Paradosis et Kyrios: Le problème de la tradition dans le Paulinisme," *RHPR* 30 [1951] 12–30; *ScotJT* 3 [1950] 180–97; *The Earliest Christian Confessions* [London, 1949]. Dodd, C. H., *The Apostolic Preaching and Its Developments* [London, 1962]. Gerhardsson, B., *Memory and Manuscript* [ASNU 22; Lund, 1961] 288–323. Goguel, M., "De Jésus à l'Apôtre

Paul," *RHPR* 28–29 [1948–49] 1–29. Hunter, A. M., *Paul and His Predecessors* [Phila., 1961] 15–57. Rigaux, B., "Le vocabulaire chrétien antérieur à la Première Epître aux Thessaloniciens," *SP* [Gembloux, 1954] 2, 380–89.)

(V) Paul's Apostolic Experience. Another factor in the development of Paul's theology was his experience as an apostle and missionary proclaiming the gospel and founding churches throughout Asia Minor and Europe. It is hard to say precisely how much his practical experience and concrete contacts with Jews and Gentiles molded his view of Christianity. But it would be wrong not at least to raise the question. Would he have written as he did on justification or on the relation of the Gospel to the Law if it were not for the Judaizing problem he encountered? The real meaning of the universal scope of Christian salvation probably dawned on him as he worked continually with Jews who failed to accept his message and with Gentiles who did heed him. From his earliest letters he reveals an awareness of the privileged position of his fellow Jews in the divine plan of salvation (see 1 Thes 2:14; cf. Rom 1:16; 2:9–10; Eph 2:13–22; 3:6). But it is only in the Captivity Letters that Paul formulates the status of Jews and Gentiles with respect to the Church and with respect to their joint relation to Christ, who is now the *kosmokrator* (to use for Christ an apt, but non-Pauline title). Such aspects of the "inexhaustible wealth of the mystery of Christ" (Eph 3:8) emerged in Paul's consciousness only as a result of intense missionary activity in the last decade of his life. The problems, too, that he encountered in founding and governing individual local churches were almost certainly responsible for his gradual awareness of what *the* Church meant (in a universal, transcendent sense). To his apostolic experience must also be attributed a number of references to the Hellenistic world, which are met in various developments of his teaching (cf. 1 Cor 8:5; 10:20–21; 12:2; Gal 4:9–10; Col 2:18–19).

(Campbell, T. H., "Paul's 'Missionary Journeys' as Reflected in His Letters," *JBL* 74 [1955] 80–92. Maier, F. W., *Paulus als Kirchengründer und kirchlicher Organisator* [Würzburg, 1961].)

Whatever Paul inherited from his Jewish background, from his contacts with Hellenism, and whatever he later derived from the tradition of the early Church and his own missionary experience was all uniquely transformed by his insight into the mystery of Christ that he acquired on the road to Damascus. Other NT writers could claim a Jewish background and Hellenistic contacts, but none of them can approach Paul's profound understanding of the Christ-event, except possibly John.

Dominant Perspectives

The key concept about which the whole of Pauline theology must be organized is Christ. Paul's theology is Christocentric. True, it is a soteriology, but his captivation with Christ makes it clear that it is a Christocentric soteriology. This may seem like a platitude, but it needs to be stressed today. Paul explicitly formulated his own message in a very similar way: "It pleased God to save those who would believe through the folly of the gospel message [kerygma]. For while Jews demand signs and Greeks look for philosophy, we proclaim a Christ who has been crucified, a stumbling block to Jews and an absurdity to Gentiles. But to those who have been called, whether Jews or Greeks, he is a Christ who is God's power and God's wisdom" (1 Cor 1:21–25, cf. Rom 1:16; 2 Cor 4:4). This "story of the cross" (1 Cor 1:18) emphasizes the centrality of Christ in Paul's gospel. Any attempt, therefore, to seek an organizing principle for his theology apart from Christ is bound to be inadequate.

This point is stressed because the otherwise excellent and justly praised exposé of Pauline theology written by R. Bultmann (*TNT* 1, 185–352) has adopted a different principle. Bultmann explains Paul's theology as an anthropology, a doctrine about man.

His exposé has two main parts: Man Prior to the Revelation of Faith, and Man Under Faith. In the *first* part (Man Prior to Faith) he discusses Paul's anthropological concepts: *sōma* (body), *psychē* (soul), *pneuma* (spirit), *zōē* (life), mind and conscience, and heart. A second section of this part is devoted to "flesh, sin, and world," which includes discussions of creation and man, *sarx* (flesh), flesh and sin, sin and death, the universality of sin, *kosmos* (world), and the law. In the *second* part (Man Under Faith) his exposé takes up the righteousness of God (the concept of righteousness; righteousness as a present reality; righteousness as God's righteousness; reconciliation), grace (grace as event; Christ's death and resurrection as salvation occurrence; the Word; the Church; the Sacraments), faith

16

(its structure; life in faith; faith as eschatological occurrence), and freedom (freedom from sin and walking in the Spirit; freedom from the law and the Christian's attitude toward men; freedom from death). These headings and subdivisions indicate Bultmann's sustained attempt to present the Pauline material in genuine biblical categories.

But such an approach is too exclusively a development of Paul's ideas in Rom, to which all else is made subservient. It reduces Paul's theology to an anthropology, whereas this is only a part of it, and not even the major part at that. In Paul's view man can be understood only in terms of the Christ-event (see Rom 7:24–8:2). In Bultmann's presentation Christ's role is minimized—not only his role in the life of individual men (since the salvific events of the first Good Friday and Easter Sunday have been demythologized to the point of being also dehistoricized)—but also his role in the corporate and cosmological dimensions of salvation history (e.g., in Rom 9–11, which Bultmann tends to neglect). This minimizing of the role of Christ stems from a refusal to admit an "objective phase" in man's redemption and a concern to recast Paul's theology in phenomenological terms. Granted that a certain amount of demythologizing of the NT has to be admitted today, yet nevertheless an exposé of Paul's theology has to reckon with the fact that he did look upon the Christ-event as the key to man's history.

(Dahl, N. A., "Die Theologie des Neuen Testaments," *TRu* 22 [1954] 21–49, esp. 38–45. Fuller, R. H., *The New Testament in Current Study* [N.Y., 1962] 54–63. Käsemann, E., "Neutestamentliche Fragen von heute," *ZThK* 54 [1957] 12–15. Marlé, R., *Bultmann et l'interprétation du Nouveau Testament* [Paris, 1956].)

If Paul's theology is predominantly a Christology, it is also important to insist on its *functional* character. Paul was not concerned about the intrinsic constitution of Christ *in se;* he preached "Christ crucified"—Christ as significant for man. "You are God's children through your union with Christ Jesus who became for us wisdom from God—our uprightness, our sanctification, our redemption" (1 Cor 1:30). This "Christ crucified," though described in figures derived from contemporary Jewish or Hellenistic backgrounds and even embellished with myth, still has relevance for men of the 20th cent. To understand Paul's thought one does not simply demythologize his description; rather the remythologization of the 20th-cent.

mind is needed in order that men might see what Paul meant and thereby understand what he means for them today. Or, to put it another way, what is needed is not subtractive, but interpretative, demythologization.

In our attempt to give a genetic development to an exposé of Paul's theology, we shall begin with the word that he himself used to describe his message about Christ, his "gospel." From such a starting point we can move on to various aspects of the content of his message.

(I) **Paul's Gospel.** *Euaggelion* as "the good news of Jesus Christ" is a specifically Christian meaning of the word and as such was almost certainly developed by Paul within the early Christian community (see W. Marxsen, *Der Evangelist Markus* [FRLANT 67; Göttingen, 1959] 83–92; but cf. E. Molland, *Das paulinische Euangelion: Das Wort und die Sache* [Oslo, 1934] 37). Paul uses it more frequently than does any other NT writer; it occurs 54 times in his letters (+ six times in the Pastorals). In general, it designates his own personal presentation of the Christ-event.

Paul did not mean by his gospel anything that resembles the Lucan Gospel. Eusebius thought that when Paul said "my [our] gospel," he meant what Luke had compiled from his preaching (*HE* 3.4, 7 [GCS 9/1.194]). This Eusebian interpretation was derived from earlier patristic descriptions of Luke's Gospel as a digest of Paul's preaching (Irenaeus, *Adv. haer.* 3.1, 1; Tertullian, *Adv. Marc.* 4.5 [CSEL 47, 431]; Origen in Eusebius, *HE* 6.25–6 [GCS 9/2.576]). But such a view of the Third Gospel is an oversimplified interpretation of Paul's expression, "my gospel"; it is the result of a facile extrapolation of the relationship between Mark and Peter. Because Luke was a companion of Paul (Col 4:14), he was believed to have been to Paul what Mark was believed to have been to Peter—a compiler of his preaching. (See T. E. Bleiben, *JTS* 45 [1944] 134–40.)

The rejection of such an interpretation of Paul's gospel, however, does not imply that when he speaks of "my gospel" (Rom 2:16; 16:25 [2 Tm 2:8]; cf. Gal 1:8,11; 2:2) or "our gospel" (1 Thes 1:5; 2 Thes 2:14; 2 Cor 4:3; cf. 1 Cor 15:1) he is announcing a gospel wholly peculiar to himself and different from those of the other apostles. He knows of only one gospel (Gal 1:6) and calls down a curse on anyone who would try to proclaim a different one (Gal 1:8).

But his gospel was not proclaimed in the form of stories about what Jesus said and did. For him, Jesus Christ is the gospel.

Paul speaks of "my gospel" because he was conscious of the special grace of the apostolate, which was accorded him to preach the good news of Christ. Like the prophets of old (Jer 1:5; Is 49:1) he considered himself destined by God from his mother's womb for this task (Gal 1:15; Rom 1:1; 1 Cor 1:17) and "entrusted" with the gospel as with some prized possession (1 Thes 2:4; Gal 2:7). He became its "servant" (*diakonos,* Col 1:23; cf. Eph 3:7) and felt a "compulsion" (*anagkē,* 1 Cor 9:16) to proclaim it. He looked on his preaching of it as a cultic, priestly act offered to God (*leitourgos, hierourgōn,* Rom 1:9; 15:16). He was never ashamed of it (Rom 1:16); rather, even imprisonment because of it was for him a "favor" (*charis,* Phil 1:7, 16). (In 2 Tm 1:10 he is described as its "herald, apostle, and teacher.")

Though Paul sometimes used the word *euaggelion* to designate the activity of evangelization (Phil 4:3, 15; 1 Cor 9:14b,18b; 2 Cor 2:12; 8:18), normally it denotes the *content* of his message—what he preaches, proclaims, announces, talks about, or teaches. These are the verbs he uses with it (see E. Molland, *op. cit.,* 11–12, 41–42). Strikingly, the content is never simply the "kingdom of God," as in Mt. His succinct expression of its content is "the gospel of Christ" (1 Thes 3:2; Gal 1:7; Phil 1:27; etc.), "the gospel of our Lord Jesus" (2 Thes 1:8), or "the gospel of his Son" (Rom 1:9). But even in such phrases the gen. may designate the author or originator too, since for Paul, Jesus is both the originator (cf. 2 Cor 5:20; Rom 15:18) and the object of the gospel proclaimed. As the content of his gospel, it is above all Jesus the Christ, the Risen *Kyrios* of all men, that Paul proclaims: "We do not proclaim ourselves, but Christ Jesus as Lord" (2 Cor 4:5); "the good news of the glory of Christ" (2 Cor 4:4). "For all the promises of God find their 'Yes' in him" (2 Cor 1:20).

Fuller formulations of his "gospel" echo the early Church's kerygma (1 Cor 15:1–7). Here he appeals explicitly to the *form* or *terms* (*tini logō*) in which he first proclaimed the gospel to the Corinthians. Significantly, the functional role of Christ is stressed: "Christ died for our sins." It recalls the Scriptures, the burial, the resurrection, and the appearances. In Rom 1:3–4 another echo of the kerygma proclaims God's son born of the line of David but set up from the time of the resurrection as a Son with power and a Spirit of holiness. The essence of the gospel is here—the emphasis on the salvific effects of the death and resurrection of Jesus the Christ in accord with the Scriptures. Paul proclaims a Son whom God "has raised from the dead, Jesus, who delivers us from the coming wrath" (1 Thes 1:10). Such a formulation of his gospel in terms of the primitive kerygma insured it against becoming a different gospel (Gal 1:6); so secured, it was the one proclaimed by the whole early Church.

But the distinctively Pauline conception of the gospel is seen in his description of it as a salvific force let loose by God in the world of man. It is not a mere series of revealed propositions about Christ that men must intellectually apprehend and give assent to. Rather, it is "the power of God [*dynamis theou*] for the salvation of every man who believes" (Rom 1:16). In other words, it not only proclaims the redemptive event of Christ's death and resurrection but is itself a force that spreads it to men. In a sense, it is itself a redemptive event whenever it makes its appeal to men. Strikingly, Paul calls it "the power of God," just as he referred to Christ himself (1 Cor 1:24). This is why to "preach Christ crucified" is to "preach the gospel." Both Christ and the gospel bring the Father's salvific bounty to men. The gospel is the Father's means of accosting men, soliciting from them the responses of faith and love. That is why it is "God's gospel" (1 Thes 2:2, 8, 9; 2 Cor 11:7; Rom 1:1; 15:16); it is also his "gift," his "favor" (2 Cor 9:14–15). So Paul can write to the Thessalonians that his "gospel was not preached to them in words only, but with power and the Holy Spirit and full conviction" (1 Thes 1:5; cf. 1 Cor 4:20). For as the "power of God," the gospel is not proclaimed without the assistance of the Spirit of God. Indeed, through this "good news of salvation" believers are sealed with the promised Holy Spirit, "the pledge of our inheritance" (Eph 1:13). Through it men are already saved (1 Cor 15:2).

Another distinctively Pauline view of the gospel is its universal appeal and application. In Rom 1:16 Paul explains it as a salvific force for "every man who believes," by adding, "for the Jew first and then the Greek." Salvation for the Gentiles through the gospel was part of his great vision of the Risen Christ—"that I might preach the good news of him to the Gentiles" (Gal 1:16). In time, Paul realized that "there is no distinction between Jew and Greek for they all have the same Lord, and he is generous to all who call upon him" (Rom 10:12; cf. 11:11, 25). Whenever Paul, then, speaks of his "gospel," it should be understood as Jesus the *Kyrios* who is the power of God for the salvation of all men, Jew and Greek alike. For even "Scripture saw in advance that God would make the Gentiles upright through faith, and announced the good news in advance to Abraham, 'In you all nations will be blessed'" (Gal 3:8).

Another aspect of the Pauline gospel is seen in his view of it as a "mystery" or "secret" (*mystērion*). This aspect introduces us more deeply into the content of the gospel, which concerns Christ, by enhancing the total view of it as a revelation. For in the gospel is revealed the divine plan of salvation, which is being realized in Christ Jesus. It is particularly in contexts mentioning the gospel as revelation or manifestation that *mystērion* occurs (note its use with the vbs. *apokalyptein, gnōrizein, phaneroun, lalein,* etc.).

The earliest Pauline use of *mystērion* (2 Thes 2:7) has nothing to do with the gospel, since it refers to the "mystery of iniquity," a satanic scheme at work in the world destined to culminate in the appearance of the "lawless one" (*ho anomos;* cf. P. Furfey, *CBQ* 8 [1946] 179–91; M. Brunec, *VD* 35 [1957] 3–33; J. Schmid, *TQ* 129 [1949] 323–43). But the first occurrences of this word thereafter reveal its identification with the gospel. Paul speaks of "God's mystery," equating it with "Jesus Christ crucified" (1 Cor 2:1–2; but cf. *app. crit.*), just as he had referred his gospel to Christ crucified (1 Cor 1:17, 23). Paul is the "steward," dispensing the wealth of this mystery (1 Cor 4:1; cf. 13:2; 14:2). His gospel is so designated because it reveals a plan of salvation conceived by the Father and hidden in him from all eternity (1 Cor 2:7). It has now been put into effect in Christ Jesus and has been revealed to Christians through the apostles and holy prophets of the New Dispensation. It embraces the salvation of all mankind, giving the Gentiles a share in the inheritance of Israel. Even the partial insensibility of Israel is part of this *mystērion* (Rom 11:25). Hidden in God for long ages, it is beyond the ken of mortal men and even of the authorities of this world. But now it has been made known "to God's holy people" and even to Paul, that he might proclaim it to the Gentiles and bring them to a share in the inexhaustible wealth of "the mystery of Christ" (Col 4:3). Although this mystery is mentioned in the Great Letters, it is above all in the Captivity Letters that Paul mani-

fests its real import, especially his insight into the cosmic significance of Christ's role. In these letters the mystery reveals Christ to
be the meaning and goal of all creation, for the Father plans to bring
all created things under the headship of Christ (Eph 1:9). Through
Christ salvation comes to all men by their incorporation in his body,
which is the Church, and he is its head (see Col 1:26–27; 2:2; Eph
1:9; 3:4–10). In Eph 3:4–10 Paul gives the fullest description of this
mystery, which dawned on him only later in his life.

The Pauline "mystery" is Christocentric. Just as Paul identifies
Christ with the gospel, calling them both the "power of God," so he
equates Christ and the "mystery," calling them "the wisdom of God"
(1 Cor 2:7; 1:24). In reality, this "mystery of the gospel" (Eph 6:19)
is one and the same: Christ is the "secret plan of God" (Col 1:27;
2:2). But in presenting the gospel as "mystery," Paul implies that it
is never fully made known to men by the ordinary means of com-
munication. As something revealed, it is apprehended only by faith;
and even when revealed, the opacity of divine wisdom in it is never
completely dispelled for men. *Mystērion* is an eschatological notion
derived from Jewish apocalyptic sources, and its application to the
gospel gives the latter a nuance that *euaggelion* alone would not
have—for it is something that is fully comprehended only in the
eschaton.

Perhaps because of his apostolic experience Paul came to speak
of the gospel as *mystērion,* using a word already familiar in contemporary Gk mystery religions. However, the comprehension he
gives to it and the mode in which he uses it reveal that he depended
not so much on its Hellenistic sources as he did on the OT and Jewish apocalyptic writings of the intertestamental period. Its OT roots
are found in the Hebr *sôd* and in the Aram *rāz* (mystery) (Dn 2:18–
19, 27–30, 47; 4:6). The latter is a Persian loanword used in Aram to
designate the revelation made to Nebuchadnezzar in his dreams.
QL offers abundant parallels to the Pauline usage of *mystērion,*
showing that its real roots are in Palestine Judaism rather than in
Asia Minor Hellenism. In QL and related writings *rāz* denotes an
eschatological secret of God, embracing creation, the history of the
world, the Endtime, and the judgment. As used by Paul, especially
in Col and Eph, *mystērion* begins with these presuppositions of Jewish apocalyptic literature, but creation, history of the world, and the

eschaton are now all involved in the great "mystery of Christ," which brings salvation to all men.

(Baker, A. E., *St. Paul and His Gospel* [London, 1949]. Brown, R. E., "The Pre-Christian Semitic Concept of 'Mystery,'" *CBQ* 20 [1958] 417–43; "The Semitic Background of the NT Mysterion," *Bib* 39 [1958] 426–48; *Bib* 40 [1959] 70–87. Burrows, M., "The Origin of the Term 'Gospel,'" *JBL* 44 [1925] 21–33. Petty, O. A., *Did the Christian Use of the Term "to Euaggelion" Originate with Paul?* [New Haven, 1925]. Schniewind, J., *Euangelion* [2 vols.; Gütersloh, 1927–31]. Vogt, E., "'Mysteria' in textibus Qumran," *Bib* 37 [1956] 247–57.)

(II) The Father's Plan of Salvation History. The nuance of "mystery" added to Paul's understanding of the gospel opens up the broad perspective in which it must really be considered. He saw the gospel only as a part of the magnificent plan, itself gratuitously conceived by the Father for the salvation of men, which was revealed and realized in Christ Jesus. This was the Father's "purpose" (*prothesis*, Rom 9:11; 8:28; Eph 1:11; 3:11; cf. Gal 4:4) and the Father's "will" (*thelēma*, 1 Cor 1:1; 2 Cor 1:1; Eph 1:5). This Pauline insight is important because it makes us aware of the historical, cosmological, and corporate dimensions of Christian salvation.

In certain quarters today this view of man's salvation is looked upon merely as the mythical element in Paul's theology. It is regarded as a prop (like God-up-there, or God-out-there), born of a supranaturalist view of the world, which is not really essential to the NT. In so far as any description of a divine plan of salvation is bound to be anthropomorphic, it can be admitted to be mythical. An effort must be made, however, to understand the myth for what it is, and not simply to reject it. The demythologization must be interpretative, not subtractive.

The author of the salvific plan is not Christ, but God the Father (*ho theos*). What Paul teaches us about the Father is not a theology (in the strict sense) independent of his soteriological Christology. It is taught, rather, in contexts that deal generally with the divine plan of salvation. "God chose through the folly of the Gospel message to save those who had faith in him" (1 Cor 1:21). The word "chose" highlights the gratuitous initiative that Paul never ceases to ascribe to the Father, whose great concern is the "salvation" of men (1 Thes 5:9; Rom 1:16; 10:10; 11:11). It is the Father who "calls" men to faith, to salvation, to glory, and even to the apostolate (1

Thes 5:24; 2 Thes 2:13–14; 1 Cor 1:9; Rom 8:30). It is a "call" that is made in virtue of an eternal plan (1 Thes 5:9; 2 Thes 2:13; Rom 8:28; 9:11; Eph 1:9, 11; 3:11). Though Paul may at times ascribe to the Father certain qualities that seem unrelated, they almost always reveal God as such and such *for us, on our behalf*, for they express aspects of his relation to the divine plan of salvation. Thus, for instance, the various attributes Paul derives from his Jewish background: God as "the creator of all things" (Eph 3:9); the one who "calls into being what does not exist" (Rom 4:17); God's "eternal power and divinity" (Rom 1:20); his "truth" (Rom 1:25; 3:7); his wisdom and knowledge" (Rom 11:33); his "wrath" (Rom 1:18); and above all his "uprightness" (Rom 3:5, 25).

If Paul speaks of the *dikaiosynē theou*, his reference should not be facilely understood of God's vindicative justice (as opposed to his mercy). Rather, this term refers to his salvific uprightness, a quality by which he manifests his bounty and fidelity in acquitting and vindicating his people. Yahweh in the OT is often depicted as the contender involved in a lawsuit (*rîb*) with his rebellious people (Is 1:18; 3:13; 41:1; 43:26; Hos 4:1; 12:2; Mi 6:2; etc.). Or else he is the "righteous Judge" (Ps 7:12). However, in the prophetic and post-exilic literature his uprightness (Hebr *ṣedeq* or *ṣᵉdāqâ*) is usually mentioned as the quality by virtue of which he "acquits or vindicates" his people (Is 43:26; 45:25; 50:8; Jer 12:1). Such an acquittal brought "salvation," and in this literature we often find Yahweh's *ṣedeq* manifesting itself as a "salvific uprightness" (Is 46:13; 51:5, 6, 8; 59:17; 45:21; Pss 36:7, 11; 143:1–2; Ezr 9:15; Neh 9:33; Dn 9:7–16). And so Paul understands it. Such qualities, then, are not meant to convey an understanding of the intrinsic constitution of God. They are, rather, an indication of God's relation to man.

(Ropes, J. H., " 'Righteousness' and 'the Righteousness of God' in the Old Testament and in St. Paul," *JBL* 22 [1903] 211–27.)

The relation of the Father to man's salvation, however, is brought out much more by the way Paul conceives of the relationship of God to Christ. For he is often, "the God and Father of our Lord Jesus Christ" (2 Cor 1:3; 11:31; Rom 15:6; Col 1:3; Eph 1:3; cf. 1 Cor 15:24). Such a conception is influenced by Paul's Jewish monotheism (cf. 1 Cor 8:5–6) but also by his insight into Christ, who is the one who reveals God to men because he is "the image of

God" (2 Cor 4:4; Col 1:15). It is the Father who has sent his Son to redeem those under the Law (Gal 4:4). The mission of the Son is the great proof for Paul of the love of the Father for men: "God proves his love for us by the fact that Christ died for us when we were still sinners" (Rom 5:8; cf. 8:31). In Christ, man encounters the supreme love of the Father. It is his love that is poured out in our hearts (Rom 5:5). It is "God who has reconciled us to himself through Christ" (2 Cor 5:18). This is the "living and true God" (1 Thes 1:9) whom Paul envisages as the author of the eternal plan of salvation and to whom he addresses his prayer (Phil 1:4; 2 Cor 1:11; 9:14–15; Rom 8:27; Col 4:3–12). (See K. Romaniuk, *L'amour du Père et du Fils dans la sotériologie de S. Paul* [Rome, 1961]; J. Levie, "Le plan d'amour divin dans le Christ selon Saint Paul," *L'homme devant Dieu* [Fest. H. de Lubac; Paris, 1964] 1, 159–67.)

Lest anyone get the impression that the mission of Christ was a sort of repair job, patching up the history of man, which had gone awry because of man's sinful rebellion, Paul insists that this salvific plan was conceived by the creator (Eph 3:9) even before the foundation of the world (Eph 1:14). After a long period in which God's patience tolerated men's sins and their neglect of him (Rom 3:23, 25; 1:21; [the period of man's "wisdom," 1 Cor 1:21; Rom 1:20; 2:14–16]), the time came when he sent his Son into the world of men (Gal 4:4) to reconcile them to himself and to give them access to himself (Rom 5:1–2, 8). All the promises of God find their Yes in Christ (2 Cor 1:20). The mystery of the gospel has revealed this salvific plan by which God would reconcile all things (men as well as other creatures) to himself in bringing about a subordination of all creatures to Christ, the *kosmokratōr*. "He made known to us his hidden purpose and will according to that design which he proposed in Christ, to realize it when the time would be ripe: that everything in heaven and on earth might be brought together under the headship of Christ" (Eph 1:9–10). (Cf. Col 1:13–20; Rom 8:28–30.) This cosmic view of Christ as the head of the universe, which is created through him, sustained in him, and finds its coherence and goal in him, comes to its fullest expression in Col and Eph. Nevertheless, elements of it appear in the earlier letters. In Rom, Paul sees all physical creation awaiting the full execution of this salvific plan. "Creation waits with eager expectation for the revelation of the sons of God. It was once subjected to frustration, through no fault of its

own; it happened through him who so subjected creation itself, and
gave it the hope that it might be freed from its bondage to decay in
view of the glorious freedom of the children of God" (Rom 8:19–
21).

Yet even this Christocentric goal of all creation is not the final
stage of the plan. The dominion of Christ, as the *Kyrios* and head of
the universe, is given to him to make clear his exalted role in the history of man's salvation. But once the divine plan has reached that
stage of the reconciliation of all men to God, "then will be the end."
Christ will "turn over the kingdom to God his Father, bringing to
an end all other government, authority and power; he must retain
the government until he puts all his enemies under his feet. . . . And
when everything is reduced to subjection to him, the Son himself
will be subjected to him who has made all things subject to him,
that God might be everything to everyone" (1 Cor 15:24–25, 28).
In such a view of the eternal plan one can see that it is the Father
from whom all things come and for whom we exist (1 Cor 8:5).
This view also explains the hierarchy of man as the head of woman,
Christ as the head of man, and God as the head of Christ (1 Cor
11:3; cf. 3:21–23; Rom 14:7–9).

Other aspects of this plan, discussed by Paul, bring out its historical and corporate dimensions. Into it, he fits the threefold division of human history already mentioned. Salvation history is divided into three great periods: (a) from Adam to Moses; (b) from
Moses to Christ; (c) from Christ to the parousia and the "end" (Rom
4:15; 5:13; 10:4). In thus dividing human history, Paul was following a similar division of the world's duration known to the rabbis.
Some of them taught that the duration of the world was 6000 years,
divided into 2000 years of *Tohuwabohu* ("unformed void"–from
Adam to Moses), 2000 years of *Torah* (from Moses to the Messiah),
and 2000 years of the *Messiah* (see *bSanhedrin* 97b; *Abodah zarah*
9b; *jMeg.* 70d; *Ep. Barnabae* 15:4). In the Messianic age the Torah
would cease (*bShabbath* 151b; *bNiddah* 61b), and the Messiah was
expected to promulgate a new Torah (*Tg. Is* 12:3; *Midr. Eccl.* 2:1;
12:1; *Tg. Ct* 5:10). (See W. D. Davies, *Torah in the Messianic Age
and/or the Age to Come* [Phila., 1952] 50–94; *Paul and Rabbinic
Judaism*, 72–73.)

Paul uses a similar threefold division of man's history. From
Adam to Moses the period was lawless; men sinned, but there was

no imputation of transgressions. Then, from Moses to Christ, the Law reigned, and men's sins were imputed as transgressions of it. Finally, the third period was begun with Christ, who is the "end of the Law" (Rom 10:4). He is its *telos*, not only in the sense that it was directed toward him (Gal 3:24), but also in the sense that he is the one who put an end to it (See Eph 2:15; Christ "abolished the Law" [*katargēsas*]). In the place of the Mosaic Law there is now the "law of Christ" (Gal 6:2), the law of the Messiah (cf. 1 Cor 9:20; Rom 13:9–10). Paul looked on the period in which he lived as that in which the "ends of the ages have met" (1 Cor 10:11), i.e., when the age of the Law met that of the Messiah. The Law indeed was only the *paidagōgos*, "slave-attendant," leading men like school-boys to Christ (Gal 3:24).

Another indication of phases of the salvific plan is seen in the role played by Israel. Privileged of old through God's promises to Abraham and to his posterity, Israel became the chosen instrument by which salvation would reach all men. "All nations will be blessed in you" (Gal 3:8; cf. Rom 4:16; Gn 18:18; 12:3). All the divine prep-arations for the Christ were made within the nation of the Jews: "To them belong filial adoption, God's glorious presence, the cove-nants, the legislation, the Temple cult, the promises, the patriarchs, and even the Messiah according to the flesh" (Rom 9:4–5). But though descended from Abraham, Israel rejected (Rom 11:15) Jesus as the Messiah and thereby apparently excluded itself from the sal-vation offered in Jesus the Christ whom Paul preached. It would seem that the divine plan had failed in its most crucial moment (Rom 9:6). Paul insists that it has not, since this infidelity of Israel was foreseen by God and was part of the plan itself. It is not con-trary to God's direction of history, since both the infidelity of the Jews and the call of the Gentiles have been announced in the OT (Rom 9:6–32). Israel's infidelity proceeds from its culpable refusal to accept him in whom a new mode of uprightness is now open to all men; but this was foreseen. It is only partial infidelity (Rom 11:1–10), since "a remnant selected by God's mercy" (Rom 11:5) has accepted Jesus as the Christ. And it is only temporary, since through Israel's false step "salvation has gone to the Gentiles to make Israel jealous. But if their false step means riches for the world, and if their failure means riches for the Gentiles, how much more will the addition of their full number mean!" (Rom 11:11–12).

Indeed, "only partial insensibility has come upon Israel, to last until all the Gentiles have come in, and then all Israel will be saved" (Rom 11:25).

(Charue, A., *L'incrédulité des Juifs dans le NT* [Gembloux, 1929] 281–333. Munck, J., *Paul and the Salvation of Mankind* [London, 1959]; *Christ & Israel* [Phila., 1967].)

This perspective of salvation history gives to Paul's Christology historical, cosmic, and corporate dimensions. It is historical, since it embraces all the phases of man's history from creation to its consummation, since it is rooted in the intervention of Christ in that history "in the fullness of time" (Gal 4:4), and since it gives that history a meaning that is not immanent in it. It is cosmic because it relates all the created *kosmos* to man's salvation in a movement of aspiration toward Christ the *kosmokratōr*, whom the Father has made its head and goal. It is corporate because it envisages the effects of the Christ-event on "the Israel of God" (Gal 6:16; cf. Rom 9:6) and because it was destined to break down the barrier between Jew and Greek, reconciling both to God in one body (Eph 2:14–16). One cannot stress too much this last dimension of the salvific plan. The corporate aspect of salvation dominates many passages in Paul, such as Rom 5:12–21; Rom 9–11; and Eph 1:3–12. It should warn us against interpreting Paul's teaching too narrowly or exclusively in an individualistic sense, either that of some I-Thou relationship between the Christian and God or, less sophisticatedly, that of a personal piety or even that of some exaggerated anthropology. This corporate aspect appears above all in the incorporation of Christians in Christ and his Church.

No sketch of Paul's salvation history is complete without some reference to his eschatology, since this complicated subject belongs, in part at least, to any discussion of the divine plan of salvation.

If the first two phases of that history (Adam to Moses, Moses to Christ) have already been brought to a close, then in a sense Christians are already living in the last age, the Messianic age. If the *eschaton* has been inaugurated, yet from another viewpoint the "end" has not yet come (1 Cor 15:24 [according to the most probable interpretation of that verse]). Christ, the *kosmokratōr*, does not yet reign supreme; he has not yet handed the kingdom over to the Father. All of this is related to the "parousia of the Lord" (1 Thes

2:19; 3:13; 4:15; 5:23; 2 Thes 2:1; 1 Cor 15:23). It is scarcely to be denied (as R. Schnackenburg rightly admits [*Neutestamentliche Theologie*, 104]) that Paul expected it in the near future. On the other hand, we find him at times in his letters gradually reconciling himself to an imminent death (Phil 1:23) and to an intermediate phase between his death and his "appearance before the tribunal of Christ" (2 Cor 5:1–10). In either case, however, there is a future phase in his salvation history, whether its term be near or far off, and Paul's one hope is "to make his home with the Lord" (2 Cor 5:8). The undeniable elements of his futurist eschatology are the parousia (1 Thes 4:15), the resurrection of the dead (1 Thes 4:16; 1 Cor 15:13ff.), the judgment (2 Cor 5:10; Rom 14:10; Eph 6:8), and the glory of the justified believer (Rom 8:18, 21; 1 Thes 2:12). But along with this future aspect there is also the present aspect, according to which the *eschaton* has already begun, and men are already in a sense saved. "Now is the acceptable time, now is the day of salvation" (2 Cor 6:2). The "first fruits" (Rom 8:23) and the "pledge" (2 Cor 1:22; 5:5; Eph 1:14) of this salvation are already the possession of Christian believers. Christ has already transferred us to the heavenly realm (Eph 2:6; cf. Col 2:12; Phil 3:20). Paul speaks at times as if Christians were already saved (Rom 8:24; cf. 1 Cor 15:2; 1:18; 2 Cor 2:15; Eph 2:8), yet at other times he intimates that they are still to be saved (1 Cor 5:5; 10:33; Rom 5:9, 10; 9:27; 10:9, 13).

This difference of viewpoint is due in part to the development of Paul's thoughts regarding the imminence of the parousia. In the Early Letters, the future references abound. But with the passage of time, and especially with some experience that Paul had in Ephesus when he came very close to death (2 Cor 1:18; 1 Cor 15:32) and the parousia had not yet occurred, his understanding of the Christian situation developed. All this is undoubtedly at the root of the full-blown vision of the Father's plan, which emerges only in the Captivity Letters.

The double aspect of Pauline eschatology has variously been explained. Some, like C. H. Dodd and R. Bultmann, would label the predominant aspect of it "realized eschatology." This expression is *in se* acceptable, but care must be exercized in defining it. For Bultmann, Paul is not interested in the history of the nation of Israel, or of the world, but only in the "historicity of man, the true historical

life of the human being, the history which every one experiences for
himself and by which he gains his real essence. This history of the
human person comes into being in the encounters which man experiences, whether with other people or with events, and in the decisions he takes in them" (*The Presence of Eternity: History and
Eschatology* [N.Y., 1957] 43). In other words, the future elements
in Paul's eschatology are only a symbolic mode of expressing man's
self-realization as he is freed from himself by the grace of Christ and
continually asserts himself as a free individual in decisions for God.
In such acts he continually stands "before the tribunal of Christ."
Bultmann would thus write off all the future elements of Paul's
eschatology listed above; they are vestiges of an apocalyptic view
of history, which is meaningless for the 20th-cent. man. Indeed, Paul
has already reinterpreted it in terms of his anthropology. "The Pauline view of history is the expression of his view of man" (*ibid.*, 41).

Such an interpretation of Paul's eschatology has the advantage
of emphasizing the "crisis" (if one will permit a word that is more
Johannine than Pauline), which the Christ-event brings into every
man's life. A challenge of faith is presented to everyone. But this
presentation of Paul's eschatology in effect denies some of the major
elements of his view of salvation history. Although it is true that
"the history into which Paul looks back is the history not of Israel
only, but of all mankind" (*ibid.*, 40), it seems hardly accurate to say
that Paul "does not see it as the history of the nation with its alterna-
tions of divine grace and the people's obstinacy, of sin and punishment, of repentance and forgiveness" (*ibid.*). Such a view of Pauline history is too much dominated by the polemics of Rom and Gal
and minimizes the problem that Paul tried to face in composing Rom
9–11. Israel's history and role in the destiny of man are factors in
Paul's whole theology; and they are scarcely a theologoumenon that
one can simply relegate to the realm of myth. Moreover, if Paul calls
Christ the end of the Law (Rom 10:4), he is not saying that "history has reached its end" (*ibid.*, 43). Rather, he would seem to be
saying that a new phase of salvation history has begun because "the
ends of the ages have met" (1 Cor 10:11).

An alternative to such a "realized eschatology" is to interpret
Paul's teaching as an "inaugurated eschatology" or even as a "self-
realizing eschatology" (if the "self" refers to the *eschaton*). For,
in Paul's view, Christians live in the *eschaton*, in the age of the Mes-

siah. This is an age of dual polarity. It is an age that looks backward to the first Good Friday and Easter Sunday and forward to a final glorious consummation when "we shall always be with the Lord" (1 Thes 4:17). It is an age that has initiated a status of union with God previously unknown and one destined to a final union in glory. This is the basis of Christian hope and patience.

Such a view of Paul's eschatology reckons with an objective mode of existence in which the Christian finds himself through faith —a mode of existence inaugurated by Christ, which will find its perfection in an event that Paul refers to as the parousia of the Lord. On the other hand, such an interpretation does not commit one to a naïve credulity that fails to reckon with the remnants of apocalyptic paraphernalia and "stage-props" used by Paul to describe the forms of the parousia, resurrection, judgment, and glory, which occur in such passages as 1 Thes 4:16–17; 2 Thes 2:1–10; 1 Cor 15:51–54.

(Guntermann, F., *Die Eschatologie des hl. Paulus* [NTAbh 13/4–5; Münster, 1932]. Hunter, A. M., "The Hope of Glory: The Relevance of the Pauline Eschatology," *Interpr* 8 [1954] 131–41. Rigaux, B., *Les Épîtres aux Thessaloniciens* [EBib; Paris, 1956] 213–22. Stanley, D. M., "The Conception of Salvation in Primitive Christian Preaching," *CBQ* 18 [1956] 231–54.)

(III) Christ's Role in Salvation History. Against the background of the gospel, the mystery, and the Father's plan of salvation, we must now try to depict the role of Christ himself as it is seen by Paul. For although Paul sees Israel and Abraham playing roles in the execution of that plan and knows that the Church is deeply involved in it, it is Christ's role that is central to his thought. This begins the Christological and soteriological part of our exposition of Paul's theology.

(A) Pre-existent Son. Paul calls Jesus "the son of God" (Gal 2:20; 3:26; 2 Cor 1:19; Eph 4:13) or "his [i.e., the Father's] Son" (1 Thes 1:10 [kerygmatic fragment]; Gal 1:16; 4:4, 6; 1 Cor 1:9; Rom 1:3, 9; 5:10; 8:3, 29, 32 ["his own son"]; Col 1:13 ["the son of his love"]). What did he mean by this title "son of God"? *In se* the title, which had a long history in the ancient Near East, could imply many things. Egyptian pharaohs were looked on as "sons of God" because the sun-god Rê was regarded as their father (see C. J. Gadd, *Ideas of Divine Rule in the Ancient East* [London, 1948] 45–50). Its use is attested also in references to Assyrian and

Babylonian monarchs. In the Hellenistic-Roman world it was used of the ruler, especially in the phrase *divi filius* or *theou huios* applied to the Roman emperor (see A. Deissmann, *LAE* 350–51). In the same world it was also given to mythical heroes or *thaumaturgi* (sometimes called *theioi andres*) and to historical persons (such as Apollonius of Tyana, Pythagoras, Plato, the Samaritan Dositheus, etc.). Abundant references can be found in G. P. Wetter, *Der Sohn Gottes* (FRLANT 26; Göttingen, 1916). The basis of the Hellenistic attribution of this title was apparently the conviction that such persons had divine powers. It has been maintained that the application of this title to Jesus reflects such a Hellenistic background, since it could scarcely have been used by Jesus himself or even applied to him by the early Palestinian community (R. Bultmann, *TNT* 1, 50). It is, however, by no means certain, as many NT scholars recognize today, that the use of this title is due almost exclusively to Hellenistic churches.

In the OT, "son of God" is a mythological title given to angels (Jb 1:6; 2:1; 38:7; Ps 29:1; Dn 3:25; Gn 6:2); a title of predilection for the people of Israel collectively (Ex 4:22; Dt 14:1; Hos 2:1; 11:1; Is 1:2; 30:1; Jer 3:22; Wis 2:16; 18:13); a title of adoption for the king (2 Sm 7:14; Ps 2:7; 89:27), for judges (Ps 82:6), for the upright individual Jew (Sir 4:10; Wis 2:18), and perhaps even for the Messiah (if Ps 2:7 is considered messianic). The hesitation in the last instance comes from the lack of any clear use of the title for the Messiah. Possible attestation of such use is found in 4Q Flor (see J. M. Allegro, *JBL* 75 [1956] 176–77), which uses 2 Sm 7:14 in an apparently messianic context. See also 1QSa 2:11–12, where God's begetting of the Messiah seems to be mentioned (cf. *JBL* 75 [1956] 177, n. 28; J. Starcky, *RB* 70 [1963] 481–505); and *Enoch* 105:2 (a later addition?). But not one of these instances is unequivocal. The identification of Messiah and Son of God is made in the NT (Mk 14:61; Mt 16:16). Cullmann believes that the fusion of the two titles first takes place here, in reference to Jesus. The dominant idea underlying the use of "son of God" in the Jewish world was that of divine election for a God-given task and the corresponding obedience to such a vocation (see Mt 21:28–31). This Hebraic notion of sonship is at the root of the NT application of the title to Christ.

Paul is scarcely the creator of this title for Christ; he inherits it from the early Church. It is found in the fragments of the kerygma that he uses in his letters. However, in his writings its meaning is not univocal. When Paul says that Jesus was "set up as a son of God in power with a spirit of holiness as of the resurrection from the dead" (Rom 1:4), he uses the title in the Hebraic sense. In this credal formulation the emphasis is on the phrase *en dynamei* (in power) which refers to the enjoyment of a plenipotentiary status as *Kyrios* ever since the resurrection (see Acts 2:36). This formulation could be no more than a sort of messianic enthronement (see L. Sabourin, *Les noms et les titres de Jésus* [Bruges, 1963] 242). It expresses the function of Jesus endowed with the life-giving spirit for the salvation of men (1 Cor 15:45). But this use of the title "son of God in power" stands in contrast to "his Son" (Rom 1:3), which seems to imply something more. Elsewhere Paul presupposes at least, if he does not allude to, the pre-existence of Christ. "God sent his son, born of a woman, subject to the Law, to redeem those who were under the Law" (Gal 4:4; Rom 8:3). Theoretically, one could say that this "sending" refers to nothing more than a divine commission. But is this all that Paul implies? The ambiguity seems to be removed by Phil 2:6, "who, though of divine status" (*en morphē theou hyparchōn;* cf. 2 Cor 8:9). The six strophes of the Jewish Christian hymn, which Paul incorporates into Phil 2, treat of Christ's divine pre-existence, his humiliation at the Incarnation, his further humiliation in death, his celestial exaltation, the adoration of him by the universe, and his new name, *Kyrios.* The status he enjoyed before the incarnation was one of "being equal to God" (*to einai isa theō*).

However, apart from such allusions to a divine dignity or to a sovereign status of Jesus as the Son, who was "the image of the invisible God, the first-born of all creation" (Col 1:15; cf. 1:17; 2:9), most of the instances in which Paul calls Jesus the "Son" express only his divine election and his complete dedication to the Father's plan of redemption. Thus, in Pauline theology it is the term par excellence to express the divine love involved in the salvation of man. With a covert allusion to the sacrifice of Isaac, Paul says of God in Rom 8:32, "he did not spare his own son [*tou idiou huiou*], but handed him over for our sakes."

One last passage needs further consideration, since Paul speaks there of the relation of the Son and the Father in a way that transcends any functional soteriology. In 1 Cor 15:24–25, 28 Paul depicts the end of the salvific plan when Christ will be sovereign *Kyrios;* but then as "the Son himself" he will be subjected to him who has put all things under his feet. Christ's role in salvation will have been brought to completion; but Paul sees the need to define the relation of the *Kyrios*-Son to the Father. Note how he uses the terms *theos, patēr,* and *huios* absolutely; Jesus is not "his son," but simply "the son."

If, then, Paul normally uses the title "Son of God" in a functional sense descriptive of the role given to Christ, there is little doubt that at times he also uses it to express something about Christ's origin and his peculiar relation to the Father. On the other hand, it is significant that only in Rom 9:5 (a textually disputed passage) do we find Paul calling Jesus *theos*. He transfers to Jesus a doxological formula otherwise reserved for the Father (Rom 1:25; 2 Cor 11:31; Eph 4:6). Possibly 2 Thes 1:12 should be added here. The reason for this rare use of *theos* for Jesus is that for Paul *ho theos* was the Father (cf. 1 Cor 8:5–6), and he is reflecting the restraint of the early Church, which though it came to acknowledge Jesus' divinity, did not, however, quickly transfer to him a title that was regarded, more or less exclusively, to be the Father's. Such restraint paved the way for the later Trinitarian dogmatic nuances. (Cf. also Ti 2:13; possibly 1 Tm 3:16 [textually problematic]; 2 Tm 4:18.)

(Benoit, P.;"Pauline and Johannine Theology," *Cross Currents* 16 (1965) 339–53. Brown, R. E., "Does the New Testament Call Jesus God?" *TS* 26 [1965] 545–73. Cullmann, O., *Christology*, 270–305. Gelin, A. [ed.], *Son and Saviour* [2nd ed.; Baltimore, 1962]. Kramer, W., *Christos Kyrios Gottessohn* [AbhTANT 44; Zürich, 1963]. Lagrange, M.-J., "Les origines du dogme paulinien de la divinité de Christ," *RB* 45 [1936] 5–33. Richardson, *ITNT* [N.Y., 1958] 147–53. Sabourin, L., *Les noms et les titres de Jésus* [Bruges, 1963] 232–44. Taylor, V., *The Names of Jesus* [London, 1953] 52–65.)

(B) Kyrios. The frequency of Paul's use of *Kyrios* for Christ is remarkable, in comparison with his use of the title "son of God," and reveals that *Kyrios* is the title par excellence for Jesus in the Pauline writings.

Paul uses *Kyrios*, of course, for Yahweh of the OT, especially in passages where he quotes or explains OT texts (1 Cor 3:20; 10:26; 2 Cor 14:21; Rom 4:8; 9:28, 29; 11:3, 34; 15:11; cf. L. Cerfaux, *ETL* 20 [1943] 5–17). In this he follows the usage of the LXX where *kyrios* is the standard rendering of *YHWH* or *'adōnai*. But the significant thing is that the absolute *ho Kyrios* becomes Paul's title of predilection for Jesus.

It has been maintained that this absolute usage is a product of Paul's Hellenistic background (by W. Bousset, *Kyrios Christos* [2nd ed.; Göttingen, 1921]; R. Bultmann, *TNT* 1, 51). The absolute use is well attested in the Hellenistic world of the Roman Empire (cf. W. Förster, *Lord* [BKW 8; London, 1958] 13–35). In oriental religious texts from Asia Minor, Syria, and Egypt, gods and goddesses like Isis, Osiris, and Serapis are often called simply *kyrios* or *kyria*. Paul himself is aware of this; though there are many "lords," yet for us there is only one Lord, Jesus Christ (1 Cor 8:5–6). *Kyrios* was also a sovereign title for the Roman emperor. Though it primarily denoted his political and juridical superiority, it also carried the nuance of his divinity, especially in the eastern Mediterranean area. However, although the absolute use of *kyrios* is attested in the Hellenistic world in the 1st cent. BC, it is not proved that Paul simply borrowed this usage and applied it to Jesus.

It is far more likely that he inherited it from the early Palestinian Church's liturgical tradition. The credal formulas of Rom 10:9; 1 Cor 12:3 point in this direction; so too does the climax of the hymn to Christ in Phil 2:6–11 (it is the name above all names given to the exalted Jesus). Compare especially Col 2:6, "you have received [by tradition, *parelabete*] Christ Jesus as the Lord." Even when writing to a Gk-speaking church like Corinth, he preserves the primitive liturgical formula *maranatha* in Aram (1 Cor 16:22). Stemming from a Palestinian community, it is affectionately retained because of its primitive connotations. Whether it should be read *maran atha* (as in A. Merk's Gk NT) and translated, "Our Lord has come" (a credal declaration), or *marana tha* (as in E. Nestle's) and translated, "Our Lord, come!" (as an eschatological prayer) is a matter of scholarly debate. The latter is usually preferred because of the translation in Ap 22:20, "Come, Lord Jesus!" (cf. *Didache* 10:6). As an eschatological prayer it implores the Lord to come in his parousia. It was probably used at liturgical Eucharistic gatherings, considered to be a foretaste of that coming (cf. 1 Cor 11:26). This evidence seems to indicate that the use of "lord" for Jesus is pre-Pauline and that it derived from the Jewish Christian community of Jerusalem.

Among the Jews of Palestine the Aram equivalent of *kyrios* was *mârê'* (emphatic, *mâryâ*). Normally, it was used of God in the form *mârî* (= *mar'î*, "my Lord"), or *mâr'an*, "our Lord," or with dependent genitives (*mârê' malkîn*, "the lord of kings"; *mârê' š°mayyâ'*, "the lord of the heavens" [Dn 2:47; 5:23]). Only in 1QapGn (20: 12–13) is an example found that is close to the Palestinian absolute use of *mârê'* for God. Data in the Gospels suggest that the disciples called Jesus *mâr'î* or *mâr'ân* at times, just as they called him *rabbî*, "my Master" (Mk 10:51). The Q source records what may be an authentic saying reflecting such a usage, "Not everyone who says to me, 'Lord, Lord . . .'" (Mt 7:21; Lk 6:46). Though the Gk text has the absolute *kyrie*, the underlying Aram was probably *mâr'î*, meaning something like "milord." Apparently it had acquired an absolute usage by this time, especially in a religious context.

This is also true of Hebr *'°dōnai*, the reverential substitute among the Jews for the ineffable name of Yahweh. In their liturgy and reading of the Scriptures it was customary to substitute for YHWH the word *'°dōnai*, "my lord," or more literally, "my lords" (a sort of plural of majesty). In the LXX, however, the absolute use of *kyrios* or *ho Kyrios* was the normal translation of YHWH, and no attention was paid to the pronominal possessive suffix on *'°dōnai*. This shows that among the Jews of the 3rd cent. BC the substitution of absolute *kyrios* for the tetragrammaton was already in vogue and that the word *'°dōnai* had already acquired an absolute connotation for itself.

Such a custom among the Jews makes it understandable how the Aram equivalent of *'°dōnai*, the title *mâr'î*, could have been applied to Jesus in the early Jewish community and still be carried over into Gk-speaking communities in the absolute form *kyrios*. Once Jesus became the object of Christian cult, the shift from the ordinary salutation *mâr'î* to a quasi-absolute use would have been inevitable. Given the absolute use of *kyrios* in the LXX for Yahweh and the contemporary application of it to gods and rulers, it was the ideal title for Paul's missionary efforts among the Gentiles.

When Paul uses *Kyrios* of Jesus, he expresses the latter's actual dominion over men precisely in his glorious, risen condition as an influence vitally affecting the lives of Christians. It does not denote Christ's role in his earthly condition, nor even his role in the eschatological parousia, but rather his present condition as the Risen Lord. It is a title of majesty given to Christ in view of his regal risen status as the Lord of the living and the dead (Rom 14:9; cf. Rom 10:9; Acts 4:12).

The use of *Kyrios* for Jesus in the early Church bestowed on him the ineffable name of Yahweh in its LXX form. In effect, it suggests that Jesus is on a par with Yahweh himself. This equality is spelled out in detail in the hymn in Phil 2:6–11; the reason why the name given to Jesus is above every name is that it is Yahweh's own name, *Kyrios*. It is the early Church's way of expressing its faith in the divinity of Christ. Though it is predominantly a functional title, expressing Christ's dominion over men and his present vital influence in their lives and conduct, yet it also denotes an equality of Christ with the Father. The titles Father and Son, being relational words, suggest distinction and even subordination. But *Kyrios* ascribes to both Yahweh and Jesus a dominion over creation and a right to the adoration of all creation. In echoing Is 45:23, Phil 2:10 implies this very idea; what Isaiah said of Yahweh is now applied to Christ: "To me every knee shall bow, every tongue shall swear."

Paul also inherited from the early Church the idea that God made Jesus *Kyrios* at his resurrection (cf. Acts 2:36, "Therefore let all the house of Israel know that God has made this Jesus whom you crucified both Lord and Messiah"). Raised from the dead through the "glory" of the Father (Rom 6:4), Christ was endowed with a "power" (*dynamis*, Rom 1:4; cf. Phil 3:10) to bring about the sanctification and eventually the resurrection of all who would believe in him. Thus he became the "lord of the living and the dead" (Rom 14:9).

Paul's awareness of the meaning of Christ's lordship grew with his understanding of the "mystery of Christ." In the Captivity Letters, Christ's cosmic role as *Kyrios* is manifest in that he has disarmed all the "principalities and powers" (Col 2:15). It is through the *Kyrios* that the unity of the Church is to be achieved: "One Lord" (Eph 4:5; cf. 2:21).

All these aspects refer to Jesus as *Kyrios* in his influence on the body of Christians. But there is an individual relationship that Paul also considers. For Paul regards both himself and the individual Christian as the *doulos*, "slave," of Christ who is the *Kyrios* (cf. Gal 1:10; Rom 1:1; 1 Cor 7:22). Yet this relationship of the Christian to the *Kyrios* is not one of despotism or tyranny; it is the very basis of Pauline "freedom"—bound over to Jesus the *Kyrios*, the Christian is

freed from self and free for others. In Gal 4:7 this is made clear in
another context ("no longer slaves but sons").

(Cerfaux, L., "Kyrios," VDBS 5, 200–28; Recueil L. Cerfaux [Gembloux,
1954] 1, 3–188. Cullmann, O., Christology, 195–237. Förster, W., Herr ist
Jesus [Gütersloh, 1924]. Förster, W. and G. Quell, "Kyrios," ThDNT, 3,
1039–94.)

(C) Passion, Death, and Resurrection. The decisive moment of the divine plan of salvation was reached in the passion,
death, and resurrection of Christ. The unity of these three phases of
Christ's existence must be retained in Paul's view of this decisive
moment. Unlike the Johannine view, which tends to make of the
ignominious raising of Jesus on the cross a majestic elevation to
glory (Jn 3:14; 8:28; 12:34) so that the Father seems to glorify the
Son on Good Friday itself (Jn 12:23; 17:1ff.), Pauline theology saw
the passion and death as a prelude to the resurrection itself. All three
phases make up the "story of the cross" (1 Cor 1:18); for it was the
"lord of glory" who was crucified (1 Cor 2:8). Though he was hu-
miliated and subjected to the powers controlling this age, his resurrection meant his victory over them as Kyrios (Phil 2:10–11; 2 Cor
13:4; Col 2:15). "He who died" is also "he who was raised up" (Rom
8:34). Although the Incarnation is a part of the salvific process (Phil
2:7; 2 Cor 8:9), Paul is not interested in it apart from the passion,
death, and resurrection. For it is in the latter phases that Jesus'
obedience is really displayed (Rom 5:19; Phil 2:8), and it is in these
phases that he manifests himself as "Son." Paul often traces man's
redemption to the gratuitous initiative of the Father who loves man
despite his sin, but he also makes clear the free, loving cooperation
of Christ in the execution of the Father's plan (Gal 2:20; Eph 5:2).
It is "our Lord Jesus Christ, who gave himself for our sins to deliver
us from the present evil age" (Gal 1:4).

The early Church recorded the memory of Christ as the Son of
Man who came not to be served, but to serve and to give his life to
free many (Mk 10:45). Paul nowhere alludes to such a saying of
Jesus (except perhaps in 1 Cor 11:24). Yet he does emphasize
Christ's voluntary, vicarious suffering and death for men. His teaching depends on the early Church's kerygma (1 Cor 15:3: "Christ
died for our sins"), echoed often elsewhere in one form or another
(1 Cor 1:13 "for you"; Rom 14:15; Gal 1:4; 3:13; 2 Cor 5:14, 21;
Eph 5:2; "Christ died for us godless men," Rom 5:6). One may at

times debate whether it should be "for us" or "instead of us," but in either case the basic Pauline message is the same. If at times Paul seems to stress the death of Christ for man's sins or for his salvation (1 Thes 5:10; Gal 2:20; Rom 3:25; 5:6,9–10) without mentioning the resurrection, he does so to emphasize the cost that this experience on behalf of men demanded of Christ. "You have been bought for a price" (1 Cor 6:20; cf. 7:22). Paul would thereby stress that it is no slight thing that Jesus did for men.

At times Paul views Christ's death as a form of sacrifice that he underwent for men or for the sins of men. This view explicitly formulated in Eph 5:2, where it is linked to the love of Christ, and where allusions are made to Ps 40:7 and Ex 29:18, "As Christ loved you and gave himself up for you as a fragrant offering and sacrifice [prosphoran kai thysian] to God." There is here no hint of propitiation, but rather an expression of Christ's love, which ascended to the Father as a fragrant sacrificial meal (cf. Gn 8:21; Dt 32:38; Ps 50:12–13). This sacrificial notion is alluded to also in 1 Cor 5:7 (Christ as the Passover lamb). The specific nuance of "covenant sacrifice" is found in the eucharistic passage of 1 Cor 11:24–25. (For the sacrificial interpretation of the highly disputed 2 Cor 5:21 [God "made him who knew nothing of sin to be hamartian"], see the lengthy discussion of L. Sabourin, Rédemption sacrificielle: Une enquête exégétique [Studia 11; Bruges, 1961]). R. Bultmann (TNT 1, 296) is probably right in saying that this view of Christ's death is not characteristically Pauline but represents a tradition that probably originated in the early Church.

What is, however, much more characteristic of Paul is the linking of death and resurrection as the salvation event. The cardinal text in this regard is Rom 4:25: "Jesus our Lord . . . was handed over to die for our transgressions and was raised for our justification." See also 1 Thes 4:14; Phil 2:9–10; 1 Cor 15:12,17,20–21; 2 Cor 5:14–15; 13:4; Rom 8:34; 10:9–10. Most of these texts leave no doubt about the soteriological value of the first Easter. Rom 4:25 itself is not an empty pleonasm, an instance of parallelismus membrorum and no more. It expresses, rather, the double effect of the salvation event: the expiation of man's transgressions (on the negative side) and the institution of a state of uprightness for man (on the positive side). Christ's resurrection was not a purely personal by-product of his passion and death. Rather, it contributed as much as these did, in a causal soteriological way, to the objective redemption of man. "If Christ has not been raised, then . . . you are still in your sins" (1 Cor 15:17). In order that Christian faith may be salvific, man's lips must acknowledge that "Jesus is Lord," and his heart must believe "that God raised him from the dead" (Rom 10:9).

It is important to note Paul's manner of speaking of the resurrection. Only in 1 Thes 4:14 does he say that "Jesus died and rose again" (as if by his own power). Elsewhere, the efficiency of the resurrection is attributed to the Father, the gracious author of the salvific plan: "God the Father raised him from the dead" (Gal 1:1; cf. 1 Thes 1:10; 1 Cor 6:14; 15:15; 2 Cor 4:14; Rom 4:24; 8:11; 10:9; Col 2:12; Eph 1:20). Christ's loving generosity is expressed in the mention of his being handed over to death, but it is God's act of prevenient favor that is emphasized when Paul attributes the resurrection to the Father. "By the power of God he is alive" (2 Cor 13:4). Indeed, we learn in Rom 6:4 that it is the power of "the Father's glory" that brought about Christ's resurrection. It was this *doxa* that exalted Christ to his glorious state (Phil 2:10). This heavenly exaltation is his *anabasis*, his ascent to the Father, just as his death on the cross expressed the depths of his humiliation and his *katabasis*. In the Captivity Letters Paul views this exaltation of the *Kyrios* as a triumphant victory-ascent over death and over all the spirit-rulers of this world (Col 2:15). It was "God's mighty strength" that was "exerted in raising Christ from the dead and seating him at his right hand in heaven, far above all hierarchies, authorities, powers, and dominions, and all titles that can be bestowed. . . ." (Eph 1:19–21). Like many in the early Church Paul saw the resurrection-ascension as a single phase of the glorious exaltation of the *Kyrios* (cf. Eph 2:5–6).

For Paul the resurrection brought Christ into a new relationship with men who had faith. As a result of it he was "set up [by the Father] as the Son of God in power with [lit., "according to"] a spirit of holiness [or sanctification]" (Rom 1:4). The *doxa* he received from the Father became *his* power, a power to create new life in those men who would believe in him. At the resurrection he became the "last Adam," the first parent of the *eschaton* (1 Cor 15:45, "The first man Adam became a 'living being'; the last Adam became a life-giving spirit"). As the "first-born from among the dead" (Col 1:18) he was, like Adam at the first creation, a principle of life for his offspring. Jesus is an instrument of a "new creation" (2 Cor 5:17; Gal 6:15) because he became at the resurrection a *pneuma zōopoioun,* a "life-giving spirit" (1 Cor 15:45). In virtue of such a dynamic principle Paul realizes that it is not he who lives any more but that it is the Risen Christ who lives in him (Gal 2:20), transforming even his physical life (cf. 2 Cor 3:18; 4:5–6). As a "life-giving spirit," Jesus brings about the justification of believers and saves them from the wrath on the day of the Lord (1 Thes 1:10; Rom 4:25). Paul prays "to know Christ and the power of his resurrection" (Phil 3:10), realizing that the *Kyrios* is possessed of a power capable of bringing about the resurrection of Christians (cf. 1 Thes 4:14).

It is through the passion, death, and resurrection that Jesus became for men a "Savior." This title, which we so frequently apply to him, is used by Paul only in Phil 3:20 and Eph 5:23; contrast the use of *sōtēr* in the Pastorals. A reason for this is that Paul normally thinks of salvation as something still to be accomplished for men by Christ (1 Thes 5:9; 1 Cor 3:15; 5:5; Rom 5:9–10; 8:24; 10:9–10, 13; Eph 3:13). Only rarely does he speak of it as something already accomplished (1 Cor 1:21; Eph 2:5, 8). If he seems to conceive of it as still being accomplished (1 Cor 1:18; 15:2; 2 Cor 2:15), the reason is that he thinks of Christ as *Kyrios* interceding for men in heaven (Rom 8:34). Paul has adapted an OT notion of salvation that is to be achieved on the "Day of the Lord [Yahweh]," on the day when faithful Israel will be saved, and the wrath of God will be manifested toward sinners.

(Durrwell, F. X., *The Resurrection: A Biblical Study* [N.Y., 1960]. Goguel, M., *La foi à la Résurrection de Jésus dans le Christianisme primitif* [Paris, 1933]. Lyonnet, S., "La valeur sotériologique de la Résurrection du Christ selon Saint Paul," *Greg* 39 [1958] 295–318. Schneider, J., *Die Passionsmystik des Paulus* [Leipzig, 1929]. Stanley, D. M., *Christ's Resurrection in Pauline Soteriology* [AnalBib 13; Rome, 1961]. Vawter, B., "Resurrection and Redemption," *CBQ* 15 [1953] 11–23.)

(D) The Lord and the Spirit. Before considering the various effects that Paul attributes to the salvation event, we must devote a few lines to the relation of the *Kyrios* to the Spirit in the Father's salvific plan. We have already seen that Paul called Christ "the power of God and the wisdom of God" (1 Cor 1:24). Like the term "spirit of God," these terms are OT ways of expressing God's outgoing activity (cf. Wis 7:25; for the "spirit of God" in the OT, see Gn 1:2; Pss 51:11; 139:7; Is 11:2; 61:1). They are periphrastic ways of describing God's active presence in the creation, providence, salvation, and the eschatological deliverance of Israel or the world. Although Paul comes to identify Jesus with the power and wisdom of God, he never calls him outright "the spirit of God."

Yet, in several places Paul does not clearly distinguish the Spirit from Jesus. In Rom 8:9–11 the terms "spirit of God," "the spirit of Christ," "Christ," and "the spirit of him who raised Jesus from the dead" are used interchangeably in Paul's description of the indwelling of God in the Christian experience. From the time of the resurrection, Christ, the "last Adam," became a "life-giving spirit" (1 Cor 15:45) and was "set up as the Son of God in power with [lit., "according to"] a spirit of holiness" (Rom 1:4). Paul speaks of the mission of the "spirit of the Son" (Gal 4:6), of the "spirit of Jesus Christ" (Phil 1:19), and of Jesus as "the Lord of the Spirit" (2 Cor 3:18). Finally, he even goes so far as to say, "The Lord is the Spirit" (2 Cor 3:17).

On the other hand, there are triadic texts in Paul's letters that line up God (or the Father), Christ (or the Son), and the Spirit in a parallelism that is the basis of the later dogma of the Trinity. (See 2 Cor 1:21–22; 13:13; 1 Cor 2:7–16; 6:11; 12:4–6; Rom 5:1–5; 8:14–17; 15:30; Eph 1:11–14, 17.) In Gal 4:4–6 there is the double mission of the "Son" and the "Spirit of the Son," and even though one may at first hesitate about the distinction of the Spirit and the Son here, there is probably an echo of the distinct sending of the Messiah and of the Spirit in the OT (e.g., Is 45:1; Ez 36:26). And 1 Cor 2:10–11, attributing to the "Spirit of God" a comprehensive knowledge of the profound thoughts of God, implies its divine character.

This double series of texts manifests Paul's lack of clarity in his conception of the relation of the Spirit to the Son. Paul shares with the OT a more fluid notion of personality than the later theological refinements of nature, substance, and person. His lack of clarity should be respected for what it is and be regarded only as the starting point of the later development. His is only an "economic" understanding of the Trinity.

As in his Christology, so too in his teaching about the Spirit, Paul is interested in the functional role played by the latter in man's salvation. If Christ opened up to men the possibility of a new life, to be lived in union with him and for God, it is more accurately the "Spirit of Christ" which is the mode of communicating this dynamic, vital, and life-giving principle to men.

Commentators have often tried to distinguish Paul's use of *pneuma* in terms of the Holy Spirit and the effects of the indwelling Spirit (see E.-B. Allo, *Première Épître aux Corinthiens* [Paris, 1934] 93–94). It may seem at times that one could prefer one meaning to the other, and thus Paul would be furnishing the basis of the later theological distinction of the created and uncreated gift of the Spirit. However, it should be recognized that this distinction is really not Paul's; the Spirit is the gift of God's presence to man, and it is better left in this undetermined state.

The Spirit is the Spirit of Power (1 Cor 2:4; Rom 15:13) and the source of Christian love, hope, and faith; it frees men from the Law (Gal 5:18; cf. Rom 8:2), from the "cravings of the flesh" (Gal 5:16), and from all immoral conduct (Gal 5:19–24). It is indeed the gift of the Spirit that constitutes adoptive sonship (Gal 4:6; Rom 8:14), which assists the Christian in prayer ("pleading with us with inexpressible yearnings," Rom 8:26), and which makes the Christian especially aware of his relation to the Father. This power of the Spirit is not something distinct from the power of Christ: Christians have been consecrated and have become upright "by the power of our Lord Jesus Christ and through the Spirit of our God" (1 Cor 6:11).

(Fuchs, E., *Christus und der Geist bei Paulus* [Leipzig, 1932]. Hamilton, N. Q., *The Holy Spirit and Eschatology in Paul* [Edinburgh, 1957]. Hermann, I., *Kyrios und Pneuma* [Munich, 1961]. Hoyle, R. B., *The Holy Spirit in St. Paul* [London, 1927]. Stalder, K., *Das Werk des Geistes in der Heiligung bei Paulus* [Bern, 1962].)

(IV) **Effects of the Salvation Event.** The effects of Christ's salvific activity are figuratively described by Paul in various ways. These effects are regarded here as part of the objective redemption, as lasting effects once produced by Christ's passion, death, and resurrection, in which man shares through faith and baptism. These effects are the reconciliation of man with God, the expiation of his sins, his redemptive liberation, and his justification.

(A) **Reconciliation.** The main effect of Christ's passion, death, and resurrection is the reconciliation of man to God, the restoration of man to a state of peace and union with the Father. This effect is *katallagē* (reconciliation), derived from the vb. *(apo)katallassō*, "to make peace" (after a war). In a religious sense these words denote the return of man to God's favor and intimacy after a period of estrangement and rebellion through sin and transgression. The idea of reconciliation underlies many of Paul's statements, but it is developed above all in 2 Cor 5:18–20; Rom 5:10–11; Col 1:20–21; Eph 2:16. By the favor of Christ Jesus, access is had by the sinner to the presence of God; he is introduced once again, as it were, into the royal court of God himself (Rom 5:2). Christ has become "our peace" (Eph 2:14), for he has broken down the party wall between Jews and Greeks—a figure derived from the barriers between the courts of the Jerusalem Temple—and abolished the Law's commandments. He has made "one new man" out of both and has reconciled them to God in one body. Through his cross hostility has come to an end, and Christ has brought "peace" (*eirēnē*) to men: "Since we are justified, we have peace with God" (Rom 5:1; cf. 2 Thes 3:16; Gal 5:22; Phil 4:7; 1 Cor 7:15; Rom 14:17; Col 3:15; Eph 2:15; 4:3). It is, moreover, a cosmic reconciliation (2 Cor 5:19), embracing "all things whether on earth or in heaven" (Col 1:20–21).

Once again, we note Paul's tendency to ascribe reconciliation to the Father. He has reconciled men to himself through Christ—and particularly through the death of Christ, "by his blood" (Rom 5:9). When we were enemies of God, we were reconciled to him through his Son's death; now reconciled, we shall be saved—indeed, we boast of God and the close union we have with him through Christ (Rom 5:10–11). The English word "atonement" aptly expresses this Christian condition—"at-one-ment" with God.

(Büchsel, F., "*Allassō*," *ThDNT* 1, 251–59. Dupont, J., *La réconciliation dans la théologie de S. Paul* [ALBO 2/23; Louvain, 1953].)

(B) **Expiation.** Paul tells us that "Christ died for our sins" (1 Cor 15:3), that "through him we enjoy . . . the forgiveness of our sins" (Col 1:14; cf. Eph 1:7). Such generic descriptions of the remission of man's sins by Christ's death or blood—a necessary condition for reconciliation—are further specified in various figurative ways. One of these is expiation.

Although the vb. *hilaskomai* (expiate, propitiate) and the noun *hilasmos* (expiation, propitiation) are used occasionally in the

NT (Lk 18:13; Heb 2:17; 1 Jn 2:2; 4:10), Paul uses only the derivative *hilastērion:* "God displayed him [Christ] as *hilastērion* with [*or:* in] his blood for the remission of men's former sins. . . ." The word *hilastērion* could be an adjective and as such would mean, "displayed Christ as expiating"; but it is more likely a noun meaning, "displayed Christ as a means [or instrument] of expiation." What is the figure Paul uses? *Hilastērion* has been explained in terms of the classical and Hellenistic Gk usage of *hilaskomai,* which with a personal object normally means "to propitiate, placate" an angry deity or hero. In a few instances in nonbiblical Greek the object is a crime or a sin, and the meaning is, rather, "to expiate." It might seem that the displaying of Christ as *hilastērion* meant that he was a means of placating the Father's anger. However, in the LXX we find God as the object of *hilaskomai* in only three places (Mal 1:9; Zech 7:2; 8:22), in none of which is there question of the appeasement of his wrath. The word is far more frequently used either of expiating sins (i.e., removing their guilt, Ps 65:4; Sir 5:6; 28:5) or of expiating some object, person, or place (i.e., performing some purificatory rite to remove its cultic defilement, Lv 16:16,20,33; Ez 43:20, 26; etc.). It frequently translates Hebr *kippēr,* which has God for its subject and seems to mean basically, "wipe away" or possibly, "cover over." The expiatory sense of *kippēr* is abundantly attested in QL (see S. Lyonnet, *De peccato et redemptione,* part 2 [Rome, 1960] 81–84). This OT and Jewish usage of the root makes it more likely that Paul has in mind some such expiatory notion rather than any appeasement of the Father's wrath. Nor should such passages as 1 Thes 1:10; Rom 5:9 be introduced to suggest that God's wrath was actually placated in the death of Christ. God's "wrath" is an eschatological notion, expressing the reaction of God to be expected on the "Day of Yahweh," when he will destroy those who have consistently resisted his will and thwarted his salvific plan by sin. It is not that God's anger has been appeased by Christ's death. It is rather that all men, Jews and Gentiles, have sinned and have fallen short of the glory destined for them. But by the favor of God, men's sins are "expiated" (wiped out, remitted) because the Father graciously saw fit to display Christ on the cross as an instrument of expiation.

But there may even be a further nuance in Paul's thought, derived from the LXX's use of *hilastērion,* where it translates the Hebr *kappōret*. The latter is often translated either as "propitiatory" (from the Vg *propitiatorium*) or as "mercy seat" (from Luther's *Gnadenstuhl*). Actually, the word may mean "cover" and may denote the "lid" of pure gold erected over the Ark of the Covenant in the holy of holies, which supported two golden cherubim, the throne of Yahweh's glorious presence in the Jerusalem Temple (Ex 25:17–22). On *Yôm Kippûrîm* (Day of Atonement) the high priest entered the holy of holies with the blood of sacrificed animals and sprinkled the "propitiatory" with it, thus atoning for his sins and for those of all Israel (Lv 16:2, 11–17). Paul may be alluding to this rite of the Day of Atonement, seeing that he mentions the "glory of God" (3:23), Christ's "blood" (3:25), the *hilastērion*, and the remission of sins (3:25). He would then be looking on Christ's cross as the new "mercy seat" and the first Good Friday as the pre-eminently Christian Day of Atonement. Christ, sprinkled with his own blood, is the real propitiatory, the Father's means of wiping out man's sins. The OT *kappōret* was but a type of the crucified Christ (see Heb 9:5). Christ was displayed in the midst of God's people as the means of blotting out their sins and giving them "access" (Rom 5:2) to the Father to whom they have thus been reconciled. (See T. W. Manson, *JTS* 46 [1945] 1–10; L. Moraldi, *VD* 26 [1948] 257–76.)

But the fuller meaning of the public manifestation of Christ "in his blood" (Rom 3:25) is understood only when a contemporary rabbinical axiom is recalled, that "there is no expiation of sins without blood" (see Heb 9:22; *Jub* 6:2,11,14; *bZebahin* 6a). The axiom itself was based on OT purificatory rites (cf. Lv 8:15, 19, 24; 9:15–16; 16:19; etc.). The idea was not that the blood so shed in sacrifice appeased Yahweh; nor was the emphasis on the shedding of the blood and the ensuing death a sort of recompense or price to be paid. Rather, the blood was shed either to purify and cleanse ritually objects dedicated to Yahweh's service (cf. Lv 16:15–19) or else to consecrate objects and persons to that service (i.e., by removing them from the profane and uniting them intimately with Yahweh, as it were, in a sacred pact; cf. Ex 24:6–8). On the Day of Atonement the high priest sprinkled the propitiatory "because of the uncleanness of the Israelites and their transgressions in all their sins" (Lv 16:16). These were considered to have defiled the land, the Temple, and all it contained. The sprinkling with blood purified and consecrated anew, expiating the sins. The underlying reason is found in Lv 17:11: "The life of the flesh is in the blood; I have put it for you upon the altar to make atonement of your lives; for it is the blood that makes atonement by reason of the life (*bannepeš*)." (Cf. 17:14; Gn 9:4; Dt 12:23.) Blood was identified with life itself because the *nepeš* (breath) was thought to be in it. When the blood ran out of a man, the *nepeš* left him. The blood that was shed in sacrifice was not, then, a vicarious punishment meted out on an animal instead of on the person who immolated it. Rather, the "life" of the animal was consecrated to Yahweh (Lv 16:8–9); it was a symbolic dedication of the life of the person who sacrificed it to Yahweh; it cleansed him of his faults in Yahweh's sight and reconciled him once more.

Christ's blood, shed in expiation of man's sins, was a willing offering of his life to bring about the reconciliation of man with God and to give him a new means of union with God (Eph 2:13). In all of this discussion of reconciliation and expiation it is important to realize how Paul insists on the gracious and loving initiative of the Father and on the love of Christ himself. Paul often says of Christ that he "gave himself" for us or our sins (Gal 1:4; 2:20; Eph 5:2, 25) and that he "loved" us (Eph 5:2, 25; Gal 2:20; Rom 8:35, 37). The same attitude toward us is ascribed to the Father (2 Thes 2:16; cf. Rom 8:32). If this element in Paul's theology is kept in mind, it will prevent one from overstressing the juridical aspects of the atonement, which certain of his expressions have at times suggested to commentators in the past. Christ's death in expiation of sin was an act of love, at once for the Father and for men, in which he made an offering of his life to rededicate men to God. Paul knows that through the death of Christ he has been crucified with Christ so that he "may live for God" (Gal 2:19). It is *not* Paul who teaches that the Father willed the death of his Son to satisfy the debts owed to God or to the devil by the sins of man.

On the other hand, it is important to recognize that Paul does at times use juridical concepts to express the various aspects of Christ's death. But they are not to be pressed to the exclusion of other aspects. In Col 2:14 Paul speaks of a "debt," which mankind owed because of its sins: God raised us to life with Christ and forgave all our misdeeds; he wiped out the debt (*cheirographon*) that stood out against us with all its items; he did away with it when he nailed it to the cross, and thus he disarmed the powers of this world.

48 DOMINANT PERSPECTIVES

This is not the image of Christ going to his death as a vicarious victim who pays the debt to the Father or the devil. It is, rather, the loving Father, recognizing the love of the Son for himself and mankind, who destroys the outstanding debt by offering his own Son. It is basically an act of God's love, which has flooded the hearts of men (Rom 5:6–8; 8:35, 39).

Lest Paul's statements, which are at times couched in juridical terminology, be forced into too rigid categories after the fashion of some patristic and scholastic commentators, it must be emphasized that Paul never specifies to whom the "price" was paid. The reason for this is that Paul did not theorize about the mystery of the redemption. He "offers to us not theories but vivid metaphors, which can, if we will let them operate in our imagination, make real to us the saving truth of our redemption by Christ's self-offering on our behalf. . . . [It is] an unfortunate kind of sophistication which believes that the only thing to do with metaphors is to turn them into theories" (Richardson, *ITNT*, 222–23).

(Dodd, C. H., *"Hilaskesthai* in the Septaguint," *JTS* 32 [1930–31] 352–60. Médebielle, A., "Expiation," *VDBS* 3, 1–262. Moraldi, L., *Espiazione sacrificiale e riti espiatori nell'ambiente biblico e nell'Antico Testamento* [Rome, 1956]. Siegman, E. F., "The Blood of Christ in St. Paul's Soteriology," *Proc. Second Precious Blood Study Week* [Rensselaer, Ind., 1960] 11–35.)

(C) **Redemptive Liberation.** Another effect Paul ascribes to Christ's salvific activity is freedom. "The glorious freedom of the children of God" (Rom 8:21) for which all creation avidly waits is not yet accomplished. But there is a freedom that Christ has already achieved for men. The classic expression for this is "redemption," a term that reflects the social institution of freeing slaves or captives. Such an institution is clearly envisaged by Paul in 1 Cor 7:23, where he counsels slaves and free men not to try to change their social status because this status matters little now that they have been "bought with a price" (7:22; cf. 6:20) and have become slaves of Christ or freedmen of the Lord. In the contemporary world of Hellenism the manumission of a slave was often a sacral affair. At Delphi and other shrines numerous inscriptions have been found that describe the manumission in terms of a fictive purchase of the slave by a god from his owner. In reality, the slave himself deposited the price of his freedom in the god's temple; it was, of course, in time turned over to his owner. But the slave was considered to have passed into the ownership of the god who thereafter protected him and guaranteed his freedom (see A. Deissmann, *LAE* 320ff.). There is a certain parallelism between some aspects of this institution and some of Paul's expressions ("bought with a price," "slave of Christ," "redemption"; cf. AG 12, 95, 205, 825). But it is at most a superficial parallelism, which needs to be modified by OT data. For it is Christ who actually pays, not the sinner-slave; as the divine purchaser, his payment is not fictive.

In the OT Yahweh is often depicted in the role of Israel's *gô'ēl*, "redeemer," i.e., the kinsman to whom fell the duty of buying back the lost freedom of a relative. This figure is applied to Yahweh in Dt-Is (41:14; 43:14; 44:6; 47:4) and the Pss (18:15; 77:35). It refers above all to the freeing of Israel from Egyptian bondage (Ex 6:6–7; Dt 7:6–8; Ps 111:9) and to the crossing of the Reed Sea (Is 43:1). Later, it is extended to Israel's return from Babylonian captivity when Yahweh brings about another Exodus of his people (Is 51:11; 52:3–9). It is noteworthy that in the OT such a "redemption" means rather "deliverance, liberation," since the payment of a *lytron* (ransom) is rarely mentioned (cf. Is 52:3). In time the notion of redemption took on an eschatological nuance, referring to what God was going to do for his people in the end of days (Hos 13:14; Is 59:20; Ps 130:7–8; Est 13:9, 16). This persists in QL (see L. de Lorenzi, *RBibIt* 5 [1957] 197–253) and the NT (Lk 2:38; 24:21). In general, it implies a deliverance from uncleanness, sin, death, and Sheol.

Another notion, however, was often linked with this redemptive liberation, viz., that of "acquisition, possession." Yahweh not only freed the Hebrews from Egyptian bondage but acquired a people for himself, especially through the covenant of Sinai (Ex 6:6–7; 15:16; 19:5; Is 43:21; Pss 74:2; 135:4). It was a deliverance, then, that terminated in "acquisition," and even in "adoption."

When Paul speaks of Christians having been "bought with a price" (1 Cor 6:14; 7:22), he is stressing the onerous burden of Christ's offering of his life for man's freedom and for the acquisition of them as "his people." In Gal (3:13; 4:5) Paul uses *exagorazō* to describe the freedom from the Law that the Christ-event has brought about (cf. F. Büchsel, *ThDNT* 1, 124–28). This rare word is never used in the LXX in a context of manumission, nor is it ever found in any extrabiblical texts referring to sacral manumission. It is a compound of *agorazō* and usually means no more than "to buy." However, it is used by Diodorus Siculus (36:2) of the buying of a slave (as a possession) and again (15:7) of the setting free of an enslaved person by purchase. In the latter context, though there is no mention of *lytron*, it is obviously a case of ransoming someone enslaved. If, then, the notion of ransom by purchase is applied to Paul's use of the word one should avoid overstressing the juridical details, since his full notion of "redemption" is colored by the OT idea of "acquisition." Paul never calls Christ *lytrōtēs* ("redeemer" = *gô'ēl;* this word is used only of Moses, Acts 7:35); nor does he ever speak of *lytron* (ransom) as such. He calls Christ Jesus "our redemption" (*apolytrōsis*, 1 Cor 1:30) in a majestic phrase that identifies the person of Christ with his deliverance and sums up a Pauline view of Christ. But it is important to note that even though it is "through the redemption which is in Christ Jesus" (Rom 3:24) that men obtain the remission of their sins (cf. Col 1:14; Eph 1:7), yet it is specifically "a redemption of acquisition" (Eph 1:14). Although redemption has in a sense already taken place (Rom 3:24), yet like the whole Christ-event it still has a future, eschatological phase, for Christians still "await the redemption of the body" (Rom 8:23). The sealing with the Spirit, which the Christian already enjoys, is only a pledge for "the day of redemption" (Eph 4:30).

The freedom Christ has won for Christians is freedom from the Law, from sin, from death, and from self (Rom 5–8). Those who were under the Law have now been bought by him; they can be called "slaves of Christ" (1 Cor 7:23; [cf. Ti 2:14, echoing Ps 130:8 and Ex 19:5]), for they owe obedience now only to him. His is the law (Gal 6:2; 1 Cor 9:21) to which they are now bound. But in him they find freedom from all the constraining elements of human existence (Gal 2:4; 4:22–31; 5:1,13; 1 Cor 9:1,19; 10:29; 2 Cor 3:17; Rom 6:18, 20, 22; 7:3; 8:2, 21), for his law is the law of love; "Love fully satisfies the Law" (Rom 13:10; cf. 8–10).

(Cerfaux, L., *Christ*, 107–10. Elert, W., "Redemptio ab hostibus," *TLZ* 72 [1947] 265–70. Lyonnet, S., *De peccato et redemptione* [Rome, 1960] 2, 24–66; "L'emploi paulinien de *exagorazein* au sens de 'redimere' est-il attesté dans la littérature grecque?" *Bib* 42 [1961] 85–89. Pax, E., "Der Loskauf: Zur Geschichte eines neutestamentlichen Begriffes," *Antonianum* 37 [1962] 239–78. Taylor, V., *The Atonement in NT Teaching* [2nd ed.; Oxford, 1945].)

(D) Justification. Another way in which Paul expresses the effects of Christ's salvific activity is by the justification of the Christian. "Jesus . . . was raised up for our justification" (Rom 4:25). This effect of the Christ-event is really not as important to Pauline theology as the Reformation controversies and Augustinian interpretation have made it out to be. It is not the key to Pauline theology, nor does it sum up the Christian experience for the Apostle—A. Schweitzer has referred to it as "a subsidiary crater." It is the aspect of salvation that emerged in the polemical context of Paul's controversy with the Judaizers. Its controversial aspect is seen when it is recalled that *dikaiōsis* (justification) is found only in Rom 4:25; 5:18 (cf. *dikaiōma*, 5:16) and that the related vb., *dikaioō*, occurs 15 times in Rom and 8 times in Gal but elsewhere only twice (1 Cor 4:4; 6:11 [cf. 1 Tm 3:16; Ti 3:7]). Moreover, it gives salvation a judicial aspect, which, though necessary for the discussion in the Judaizing context, hardly epitomizes the Christian reality itself. However, there is a positive value in the aspect of justification when it is properly interpreted, i.e., as a manifestation of the "uprightness of God" as this term was understood in the prophetic and post-exilic OT literature and other late Jewish writings. (See further K. Stendahl, "The Apostle Paul and the Introspective Conscience of the West," *HarvTR* 56 [1963] 199–215.)

Justification as a metaphor applied to salvation is derived from a judicial procedure that issues a verdict of acquittal; and it is almost exclusively a Pauline view of salvation. But for an understanding of what is really meant by it, its OT roots must be considered. We have already mentioned the "uprightness of God" (see page 24); it is that quality by which Yahweh as the judge of Israel manifests his salvific bounty toward his people in a just decision. It is a quality related to his covenant mercy (*hesed*); in the LXX, *dikaiosynē* often replaces *eleos* as the translation of *hesed* (Gn 19:19; 20:13; 21:23; 24:27; etc.). This shows how it came to designate "favor toward Israel," without, however, losing completely its basic judicial connotation. If certain circles in late Judaism tended to forget about this comprehensive view of "God's uprightness" (as Paul's Judaizing adversaries seem to have done), the notion was preserved at least among the Essenes of Qumran. Abundant references are found in QL to *ṣedeq 'El* or *ṣidqat 'El*, which are understood in a fashion that is strikingly close to the Pauline "uprightness of God" (cf. 1QS 11:4–9,11–13,18; 1QH 9:33; 1:6–9; 14:15–16).

(Benoit, P., "Qumrân et le Nouveau Testament," *NTS* 7 [1960–61] 276–96, esp. 292–95. Braun, H., "Qumrân und das Neue Testament," *TRu* 29 [1963] 189–94. Nötscher, F., *Zur theologischen Terminologie der Qumrân-Texte* [BBB 10; Bonn, 1956] 158–64. Schulz, S., "Zur Rechtfertigung aus Gnaden in Qumrân und bei Paulus," *ZThK* 56 [1959] 155–85.)

The manifestation of this divine attribute forms the theme of the first part of Rom (see 1:17, contrasted with God's wrath; cf. 3:21, 22, 25, 26; 10:3). Because Yahweh is upright, it is he who justifies man (cf. Rom 3:26; 8:33).

The OT taught that "no living man is upright before God" (Ps 143:2), i.e., achieves by himself a status of acquittal in God's sight (cf. 1 Kgs 8:46; Jb 9:2; Ps 130:3–4; Is 64:6). The justification of man was expected to be brought about by a coming redeemer (Is 59:15–20). But Paul stresses that the justification has already taken place through faith in the Christ-event: "It was to show forth now at the present time that he [God] is upright himself, even in making upright the man who has faith in Jesus" (Rom 3:26; cf. 5:1). Not only does Paul emphasize that the justification of man has already come about, but he insists on the utter gratuity of it. It comes only from God. For their part, men have "sinned and fall short of the glory of God" (Rom 3:23), but God out of sheer favor has brought it about through Christ that man stands upright before God.

This justification as a divine act implies a declaration that sinful man is upright before God. Does this mean that he is merely declared to be so—when he is really a sinner—by some legal fiction? We might expect that *dikaioō*, like other Gk verbs ending in *-oō*, would have a causative, factitive meaning: "to make someone *dikaios*" (cf. *douloō*, "enslave"; *nekroō*, "mortify"; *anakainoō*, "renew"; etc.). But in the LXX, *dikaioō* seems normally to have a declarative, forensic meaning. At times this seems to be the only sense intended in Paul's letters (cf. Rom 8:33); but many instances are ambiguous. One can certainly not appeal to this forensic sense to exclude a more radical transformation of man through the Christ-event, making it the essence of the Christian experience, as it were. For justification is really the placing of man in a status of uprightness in the sight of God through the association of him with the salvific activity of Christ Jesus—through the incorporation of him in Christ and his

Church through faith and baptism. The result of this justification is that the Christian becomes *dikaios* (upright); he is not just declared to be so but is actually constituted such (*katastathēsontai*, Rom 5:19). Paul recognizes that as a Christian he no longer has an uprightness of his own, based on the Law, but one acquired through faith in Christ, an "uprightness from God" (Phil 3:8–9). And the Christian in union with Christ is even said to become "the uprightness of God" (2 Cor 5:21).

(Bultmann, R., "*Dikaiosynē Theou,*" *JBL* 83 [1964] 12–16. Descamps, A., *Les justes et la justice* [Louvain, 1950]. Descamps, A. and L. Cerfaux, "Justice," *VDBS* 4 [1949] 1417–1510. Jeremias, J., "Justification by Faith," *The Central Message of the New Testament* [London, 1965] 51–70. Käsemann, E., "God's Righteousness in Paul," *Bultmann School of Biblical Interpretation: New Directions?* [Torchbooks 251L; N. Y., 1965] 100–110. Lyonnet, S., "De 'justitia Dei' in Epistola ad Romanos," *VD* 25 [1947] 23–34, 118–21, 129–44, 193–203, 257–63. Quell, G. and G. Schrenk, *Righteousness* [BKW 4; London, 1951]; "*Dikaiosyne,*" *ThDNT* 2, 174–225. Tobac, E., *Le problème de la justification dans Saint Paul* [Louvain, 1908].)

(V) Man Before Christ. What effect does the Christ-event actually have on the lives of men? How do men share in the redemption brought by Christ? Having sketched the objective aspects of Christian salvation, we now pass to a discussion of the ways in which Paul sees men affected by what Christ did. To understand the Pauline view of the Christian experience from the side of man, we must look at the way Paul regarded man before Christ's coming. His view is at once corporate and individual. We now touch upon Paul's anthropological views.

The corporate view of man's state before Christ should be sketched first because it is more closely related to salvation history than is the individual view. Paul often contrasts what man's situation once was with what it is "now" in the Christian dispensation (cf. Gal 4:8–9; 1 Cor 6:11; Col 1:21–22; 3:7–8; Eph 2:1–6; 2:11–13; 5:8).

(A) Sin. In the period before Christ men were sinners who, despite their strivings to live uprightly, never achieved that goal and never reached the destiny of glory intended for them (Rom 3:23). Paul's indictment of the Gentiles' ungodliness and wickedness, which suppressed the truth in their lives, is severe (Rom 1:18–23). He finds that they have no excuse for not honoring and thanking God as a result of what they knew about him in his creation, apart from

God's OT revelation of himself. "In not knowing God," the Gentiles "were in bondage to beings that were no gods . . . and were slaves to elemental spirits" (Gal 4:8–9). Their condition of servitude did not enlighten them about their degraded conduct (Rom 1:24–32; 1 Cor 6:9–11). But the picture is not wholly black, for Paul admits that Gentiles did at times fulfill some of the prescriptions of the Mosaic Law (Rom 2:14), "being a law to themselves," i.e., being aware through their consciences of what the Mosaic Law positively prescribed for Jews.

As for the Jews, who gloried in the possession of the Mosaic Law as a manifestation of Yahweh's will and as a guide for their conduct, Paul's indictment of them is equally telling. They may have the Law, but they do not observe it. Not even their practice of circumcision or their possession of the oracles of salvation can save them from the wrath befitting sin (Rom 2:1–3:8).

Without the gospel the whole human race, "all men, both Jews and Greeks, are under the power of sin" (Rom 3:9). Men find themselves in a condition of hostility toward God (Rom 5:10), being dedicated neither to his honor and service (Rom 1:18) nor to honoring his name (Rom 2:24). Their condition is an estrangement from God and a bondage to Satan (Eph 2:2; 6:11–12; Col 1:13), a form of "death" (Eph 2:1, 5; Col 2:13).

Paul at times refers to sin in such a way that one might consider it a "debt" to be remitted (Rom 3:25; Col 1:14; 2:14; Eph 1:7), but more frequently he treats it as a force or power that has invaded man and is abetted by all his natural inclinations. The individual sinful acts of man are "transgressions" (Gal 3:19; Rom 2:23; 4:15), "trespasses" (Gal 6:1; Rom 5:15, 16, 17, 18, 20), and "sins" (Rom 3:25 *hamartēmata*). But *hamartia* is an active evil influence in man's life, pervading his whole history. Both Sin and Death are personified by Paul and perform as actors on the stage of man's history. Sin was introduced into the history of mankind by Adam's transgression and brought Death in its wake (in a total sense: physical death leading to spiritual death).

In his teaching on the pervasive influence of Sin in the world before Christ, Paul depends on the OT and current Jewish ideas about the character of Sin and Death. Genesis 2–3 expressly depicts Adam and Eve's loss of trusted intercourse and friendship with God and the consequent labor, pains, and death that are their lot. The unmistakable etiological character of the narrative implies that the sin of Adam and Eve was the cause of all human misery. Yet neither in Gn nor anywhere else in the early books of the OT is this connection definitely established. It is not until the late Book of Sirach (*ca.* 190 BC) that corporal death is presented as a hereditary(?) consequence of the sin in Eden: "Sin began with a woman and because of her we all die" (25:24). In Wis 2:23–24 we read, "God created man for immortality and made him the image of his own eternity, but through the devil's envy death came into the world." Yet even in this text death is not merely physical, corporal death.

The OT teaches the general sinfulness of man in many places (Gn 6:5; 8:21; Jb 4:17; 14:4; 15:14; Pss 120:3; 143:2). This teaching, however, is presented as the datum of experience; all men are known to sin. The few texts that might suggest a sinful disposition in man (Gn 8:21; Jb 14:4; Ps 51:7) express in reality only an inclination to sin, which is almost innate. They hardly give expression to a belief in a sinful condition inherited from Adam and Eve. Again, in Jewish intertestamental literature many passages refer death to Adam or Eve (*2 Enoch* 30:17, "I created him a wife, that death should come to him by his wife"; *Apoc. Mos.* 14, "Adam said to Eve, 'What have you done to us in bringing on us the great wrath [death] which now rules over our whole race?' "; cf. *2 Esdras* 3:7). But even in this literature no unequivocal passage is found that ascribes hereditary sin to Adam or Eve. The closest one comes to this notion is in *Apoc. Mos.* 32: "All sin has come through me into creation." Yet even this statement only asserts that Eve was the first sinner (cf. Josephus, *Ant.* 3.8, 1 §190; Philo, *De vita Mos.* 2.147). The Psalmist of Qumran sings, "And he [man] is in iniquity from the womb" (1QH 4:29–30), which expresses again only the complete sinfulness of man's existence.

Paul clearly echoes the Jewish tradition of hereditary death, ascribing the situation to Adam (1 Cor 15:21–22: "all men die in [*or* through] Adam"). Since in the context the contrast is with resurrection to life (eternal), Paul is thinking of total death (which includes, of course, physical death). The connection of death with Adam is not explained in 1 Cor, but in Rom 5:12 the death of all men is attributed to Adam because of his sin: "Just as through one man Sin entered the world, and through that Sin, Death—and in this way death passed to all men, inasmuch as all men sinned. . . ." In this verse Paul ascribes to Adam not only the condition of total death, which affects all men, but also the condition of sin, which also affects all men, and this independently of their own personal transgressions. This sense is not derived from some "habitual" meaning of *hēmarton*, nor from the phrase *eph'hō* understood of some incorporation of all men in Adam. The context (vv. 13ff.) rather demands such a notion, and especially 5:19: "Just as that one man's disobedience made (*katestathēsan*) the mass of mankind sinners, so this one's obedience will make the mass of them upright." The contrast of antitype and type, Christ and Adam, would demand that the sinful condition of all men be due to Adam (independently of their own sins, which also lead to death), just as the condition of uprightness is due to Christ alone.

> (Barrett, C. K., *From First Adam to Last: A Study in Pauline Theology* [London, 1962]. Barrosse, T. A., "Death and Sin in Saint Paul's Epistle to the Romans," *CBQ* 15 [1953] 438–59. Brandenburger, E., *Adam und Christus* [WMzANT 7; Neukirchen, 1962]. Bultmann, R., "Adam und Christus nach Rm 5," *ZNW* 50 [1959] 145–65. Dubarle, A.-M., *Original Sin: The Biblical Doctrine* [N.Y., 1965]. Freundorfer, J., *Erbsünde und Erbtod beim Apostel Paulus* [Münster, 1927]. Ligier, L., *Péché d'Adam et péché du monde*, vol. 2 [Coll. Théologie 48; Paris, 1961].)

(B) The Law and the Spirits. Man's condition before Christ was not only a bondage to Sin and Death but an enslavement to the "spirits" of this world and to the Law. "In your ignorance," Paul says to former pagan Galatians, "you were slaves to gods that really did not exist" (Gal 4:8). It is a matter of disputed interpretation whether these "gods" were the spirits that bore the title of "elements of this world" (Gal 4:9; cf. Col 2:20), "thrones, dominions, principalities, authorities" (Col 1:16; cf. Eph 1:21)—or "whatever title has been given to them." At times one wonders if Paul really believed in their existence. He scoffs at them as he asserts the supremacy of Christ (Col 2:10, 15, 18; Eph 3:10). But at times he ascribes man's sinful condition to the "course of this world, to the prince of the realm of the air" (Eph 2:2; cf. Eph 6:12). He envisages the possibility of "angels" being hindrances to the love of God in Christ (Rom 8:38), announcing another gospel different from his own (Gal 1:8). That the angels were the promulgators of the Mosaic Law that enslaved men is a sign of its inferiority to the promises of God (Gal 3:19). Such spirits are not always evil; they may be good or at least neutral (1 Cor 11:10; Gal 4:14). But if they have held sway over men till now, their rule has been broken in the coming of the *Kyrios*, Jesus Christ. Because of him even Christians will now judge the angels (1 Cor 6:3), so completely is their sway over men undone.

But men were enslaved to the Law as well as to the angels. Paul now thinks in terms of Israel's history (see Gal 4:3–5, 8–9; 5:1–3; Rom 7:1ff.). Except for a few passages where *nomos* is qualified either explicitly (Rom 3:27, "law of faith"; 8:2, "law of the Spirit"; 8:7, "law of God"; Gal 6:2, "law of Christ") or by the context (playing on the idea of *nomos*, Rom 2:14b; 7:2–3, 21–25), *ho nomos* or simply *nomos* otherwise always means for Paul the Mosaic Law, without any distinction being made between cultic or ritual commandments and ethical requirements (cf. Gal 4:10; 5:3; Rom 7:7). He occasionally speaks of *entolē*, but this word denotes only a "commandment," a way of designating the whole by a part. (See R. Bultmann, *TNT* 1, 260–61; H. Kleinknecht and W. Gutbrod, *Law* [BKW 11; London, 1962] 101.) One should beware, then, of interpreting *nomos* without the article in terms of "law in general." (Cf. G. B. Winer, *Grammatik des NT Sprachidioms* [8th ed.; Göttingen, 1894] §19, 13h; Bl-Deb-F §258.2.)

As Paul personified Sin and Death, so he also personified Law (*nomos*; cf. Rom 7:1). All three are actors on the stage of man's history, playing their roles of *kyrioi*. Because of Adam's transgression Sin and Death entered the world. But men began to sin in imitation of Adam only when the Mosaic Law came upon the stage, bringing with it a "real awareness" of what sin is (Rom 3:20).

Paul recognized that the Law in itself was "good, just and holy" (Rom 7:12, 16 [cf. 1 Tm 1:8–9]). He even calls it *pneumatikos*, "related to the Spirit," because it comes from God (7:14, 22, 25; 8:7). It was destined to lead men to life (Rom 7:10; cf. Gal 3:12) and was in no way a contradiction of God's promises (Gal 3:21). It was addressed to those under its authority (Rom 3:19); yet it did little good for a Jew to boast of possessing it without obeying it (Rom 2:12–13, 17–18, 23, 25; 9:4). Uprightness was sought by doing the "deeds of the Law."

Yet the Law could not produce the uprightness it was supposed to. Paul was firmly convinced of this; he quotes Ps 143:2, "No human being will be justified before him," and explicitly adds, "by deeds of the Law" (Rom 3:20; cf. 3:21, 28; 8:3). In Gal he expressed the same idea in terms of "life" (3:12, quoting Hab 2:4). In spite of the Law the Jews were as much sinners as were the Gentiles (Rom 2:17–24). The reason was because the Law provided merely an extrinsic norm for what should be done without supplying any *dynamis* (power) to do it.

As a result, the Law multiplied sin (Gal 3:19; Rom 5:20; 7:13). Not only did it become the *dynamis* of Sin (1 Cor 15:56), making man liable to God's wrath (Rom 4:15), but it positively aided sin, even though it was not sin in itself (Rom 7:7). The Mosaic Law proved to be an occasion for sin because it either instructed man in the material possibilities of sin by forbidding something which was in itself indifferent, or it excited his concupiscence into going after forbidden fruit (Rom 7; 5, 8, 11). But much more important was its role as moral informer, for the Law gave man a "real awareness" (*epignōsis*) of sin (Rom 3:20), i.e., the understanding of a moral disorder as transgression and rebellion against God. Such an awareness did not exist in the world before Moses (Rom 5:13; 4:15). "Without the Law Sin was dead . . . but when the commandment came, Sin revived and I died" (Rom 7:8–9). Sin was shown up by it in its true colors.

But worse still, it laid a curse on all who did not observe it: "Cursed be anyone who does not stand by everything that is written in the book of the Law and obey it" (Gal 3:10, quoting Dt 27:26). As the instrument and accomplice of Sin, the Law that should have meant life for man proved to mean only death (Rom 7:10). It brought down on him a "condemnation" (Rom 8:1); it was a "dispensation of death" (2 Cor 3:7), a "dispensation of condemnation" (2 Cor 3:9), and the "letter that kills" (2 Cor 3:6).

Paul sensed the anomaly of the stern accusations he brought against Mosaic Law, which came from God. "Did what was good then prove the death of me? Certainly not! It was Sin that did so, that it might be recognized as sin" (Rom 7:13). The Law was but the tool of *hamartia*. But in using the Law, Sin's true character was revealed.

How could God have permitted what was "good, just, and holy" to serve such a cause? Paul explains the anomaly in two ways. First, in Gal he explains that the Law was temporary. Before faith came, men were imprisoned under the Law "in order to obtain the faith to be revealed" (Gal 3:23). The Law acted as a slave-attendant (*paida-*

gōgos) leading men to Christ. The sense of this role is not that a man can only attain true faith in Christ when his self-righteousness has been crushed by the Law or when he has been made by the Law to feel his desperate need for a savior. In the framework of salvation history the Law plays the role of leading men to find their salvation through faith in Christ. To the promises of salvation that had been made to Abraham the Law was added some 430 years later and was promulgated by angels through the mediation of Moses. All of this manifests its temporary, inferior character in God's salvific plan (Gal 3:17–20); it was but a facet of Israel's role in that plan. Second, in Rom Paul explains that the anomaly is really due to man, who is *sarkinos,* "made of flesh." The *egō* is not simply identified with Sin and Flesh. But though the Law came from God and was *pneumatikos,* it did nothing to resolve the conflict that every man experiences, especially since every man is "sold under sin" (Rom 7:14). Though "in his inmost self he delights in the law of God" (Rom 7:22), he knows that "Sin dwells in him" (7:17). Paul figuratively even calls this sin "another Law" (7:23). So, once again Paul lays the blame not on the Law but on Sin and on man's inability to do the good that he would (7:15). But the Law did not help him to resolve this predicament. (See K. Stendahl, *HarvTR* 56 [1963] 199–215.)

The anomaly was, however, resolved in Christ Jesus and in him alone. "This is the freedom for which Christ has freed us" (Gal 5:1), a freedom from the Law's regime. "Through the body of Christ you have become dead to the Law" (Rom 7:4). It is Christ too who saved men from enslavement to Sin and Death. "Who can save me from this doomed body [lit., "body of death"]? Thank God! It is done through Jesus Christ our Lord" (Rom 7:25). "There is condemnation no more for those in union with Christ Jesus. The life-giving law of the Spirit has freed you through Christ Jesus from the law of sin and death" (Rom 8:1–2). "You are no longer under the Law but under grace" (Rom 6:14). Thus, Christ is the "end of the Law" (Rom 10:4). The Christian has died to the Law because through baptism he has been crucified with Christ, who was put to death "through the [Mosaic] Law" (Gal 2:19). The mentality induced by the Law could not accept Jesus as the Christ and actually did away with him. But the very death of Christ was the liberating act whereby the curse of the Law was broken. Though he was born under the Law (Gal 4:4) and was sinless (2 Cor 5:21), he was eventually brought to the condition where a curse of the Law fell on him too—the curse of Dt 21:23, which was leveled against a dead body exposed on a tree. The connection between the two curses is only extrinsic and material, but Paul, using a principle of rabbinical logic, saw in the curse of Christ the means whereby the curse of the Law upon men was removed.

How did Paul arrive at such a negative view of the Law? Does he not seem to be a Marcionite after all? Faced with this problem, commentators have sometimes tried to say that Paul was referring to the cultic and ritual parts of the OT. This is an inadequate explanation, since Paul refers to the Decalogue explicitly in Rom 7:7. It does not help to say that Paul is talking about "law in general" (i.e., any legalistic system). Part of the problem is that Paul viewed the OT often through Pharisaic and rabbinical glasses and was preoccupied with its 613 commands and the casuistic interpretations of the Fathers that explained them. He rarely refers to the OT as covenant (see the fleeting references in Rom 9:4; Eph 2:12; 2 Cor 3:14; Gal 3:17 [the covenant of promise made with Abraham, not the great event of Sinai!]). This may be the result of Paul's dependence on the LXX in which the notion of the Hebr $b^e r\hat{\imath}t$ was translated by $diath\bar{e}k\bar{e}$, a word that in Hellenistic times meant "last will, testament" (cf. Gal 3:15). It obscured the covenant as a $synth\bar{e}k\bar{e}$ (pact) and gave it the sense of God's will that had to be executed by Israel.

Whatever the real answer to this problem of Paul's view of the Mosaic Law is, he was convinced that a new way of life had been introduced into man's history by Christ's death and resurrection. It was no longer a "law of deeds" that man must perform, but a "law of faith" (Rom 3:27). Man finds himself freed from the Law in Christ, whereas before Christ he was enslaved to it. He is freed from that which constrained and coerced him from without but that gave him no assistance to do the good that it ordered.

(Benoit, P., "La loi et la croix d'après Saint Paul," *RB* 47 [1938] 481–509. Berkhof, H., *Christ and the Powers* [Scottsdale, Pa., 1962]. Bläser, P., *Das Gesetz bei Paulus* [NTAbh 19/1–2; Münster, 1941]. Branscomb, B. H., *Jesus and the Law of Moses* [London, 1930]. Caird, G. B., *Principalities and Powers* [Oxford, 1956]. Lyonnet, S., "St. Paul: Liberty and Law," *The Bridge* 4 [1961–62] 229–51. Reicke, B., "The Law and This World According to Paul," *JBL* 70 [1951] 259–76. Schlier, H., *Principalities and Powers in the NT* [Freiburg, 1961].)

(C) **Man.** One of the problems that Paul tried to explain in his picture of man before Christ is the makeup of man himself. Man's inability to observe the Mosaic Law stems in part from his condition as *sarkinos*. What does Paul mean by this? To explain we must try to ascertain what he meant by *sōma* (body), *sarx* (flesh), *psychē* (soul), *pneuma* (spirit), *kardia* (heart), and *nous* (mind). Paul does not really describe for us man *in se* but describes, rather, different relations of man vis-à-vis God. These terms, then, do not really designate parts of man but designate, rather, aspects of the whole man as seen from different perspectives.

A popular, common conception of man as made up of two parts is found at times in Paul's writings (1 Cor 5:3; 7:34; 2 Cor 12:2–3). The visible, tangible, biological part made up of members is called *sōma* (Rom 12:4–5; 1 Cor 12:12–26). Though at times he seems to mean by it only the flesh and bones of man (Gal 1:16; 1 Cor 13:3; 2 Cor 4:10; 10:10; Rom 1:24), he normally means far more. Man does not merely have a *sōma*, he is a *sōma*. It seems to be Paul's way of saying "self" (Phil 1:20; Rom 6:12–13; cf. 1 Cor 6:15 and 12:27). It denotes man as a whole, as a unified, complex living organism, even as a person, especially when he is the subject to whom something happens or is the object of his own action (1 Cor 9:27; Rom 6:12–13; 12:1; 8:13; cf. R. Bultmann, *TNT* 1, 195). A corpse is not a *sōma*, and there is no form of human existence for Paul without a body in this full sense (see Phil 3:21; 1 Cor 15:35–45; 2 Cor 5:2–4; but cf. 2 Cor 12:2–3; 5:6–8). When Paul uses *sōma* in a pejorative sense, when speaking of the "desires or passions" of the body (Rom 6:12; 8:13), of the "body of sin" (Rom 6:6), of the "body of humiliation" (Phil 3:21), or of "the body of death" (Rom 8:3), he really means man under the sway of some power like Sin, or the "flesh" (Rom 7:14, 18, 23; 8:3, 13). In these cases, *sōma* is the sin-ruled self (Rom 7:23), and this self is the condition of man before the coming of Christ—or even after the coming of Christ, if he does not live in Christ.

In the OT the word *bāśār* expressed the idea of both "body" and "flesh." Paul reflects this OT notion when he uses *sarx* as a synonym for *sōma* (1 Cor 6:16, quoting Gn 2:24; 2 Cor 4:10–11; cf. Gal 4:13; 6:17). In these cases *sarx* means the physical body. The phrase, "flesh and blood," designates man (Gal 1:16; 1 Cor 15:50; Eph 6:12) and connotes his natural frailty as a human being. It is a late OT expression (Sir 14:18; 17:31). But *sarx* alone can also denote humanity or human nature (Rom 6:19; 3:5; 1 Cor 9:8). However, the more typically Pauline use of *sarx* denotes man in his natural, physical, and visible existence, weak and earthbound (*ta melē ta epi tēs gēs,* Col 3:5); it connotes the natural human creature left to himself. "No flesh can boast of anything before God" (1 Cor 1:29). "People who are controlled by the flesh think of what·pertains to the flesh" (Rom 8:5); they cannot please God (Rom 8:8). The "deeds of the flesh" are retailed in Gal 5:19–21; it should be superfluous to note that for Paul "flesh" is not restricted to the area of sex. Paul can identify the *egō* and *sarx* and find no "good" in them (Rom 7:18). *Sarx* denotes, therefore, the whole man dominated by natural, earth-oriented tendencies. This notion is prominent in the famous Pauline contrast of "flesh" and "spirit," which compares man subject to his earthly tendencies with man under the influence of the Spirit. *Sarx* is man in his contrast to God, subject to all that withdraws him from God.

Similarly, *psychē* is not just the vital principle of biological activity in man. As in the OT, it denotes a "living being, living person" (Hebr *nepeš;* 1 Cor 15:45). It expresses man with his vitality, his consciousness, his intelligence and volition (1 Thes 2:8; Phil 2:30; 2 Cor 1:23; 12:15; Rom 11:3; 16:4). Even when it seems to mean nothing more than "self" (Rom 2:9; 13:1), there is always the connotation of conscious, purposeful vitality, of "life." And yet it is only the earthly, natural "life" of man. Normally, Paul does not use *psychē* in a derogatory sense; but it is, on the other hand, clearly the life of *sarx* and not the life dominated by the Spirit. This is why he calls the man *psychikos* who lives without the Spirit of God (1 Cor 2:14). This is "material" man, not "spiritual" man (*pneumatikos*).

In 1 Thes 5:23 Paul lines up what seems to be three parts of man: *sōma, psychē,* and *pneuma*. In this case *pneuma* is not the Holy Spirit (cf. Rom 8:16; 1 Cor 2:10–11). Joined to *sōma* and *psychē,* which denote the whole man under different aspects, *pneuma* would seem to be another aspect. But it is not always easy to distinguish *pneuma* in this sense from *psychē* (cf. Phil 1:27; 2 Cor 12:18). If anything, *pneuma* suggests the knowing and willing self of man and as such reveals him to be particularly apt to receive the Spirit of God. Sometimes, however, it is a mere substitute for the personal pronoun (Gal 6:18;~2 Cor 2:13; 7:13; Rom 1:9; Phlm 25).

Nous for Paul seems to describe man as a knowing and judging subject; it designates his capacity for intelligent understanding, planning, and decision (cf. 1 Cor 1:10; 2:16; Rom 14:5). In Rom 7:23 it is the understanding self that hears God's will addressed to it in the Law and that agrees with God's will and accepts it as its own. It is this capacity of man that recognizes what can be known about God from his creation (Rom 1:20); the *nooumena* are the things that the *nous* can grasp. There is really little difference in Paul's use of *nous* and *kardia* (heart), which, as in the OT, often means "mind." If anything, *kardia* would connote the more responsive and emotional reactions of the intelligent, planning self. For it "loves" (2 Cor 7:3; 8:16), "grieves" (Rom 9:2), "plans" (1 Cor 4:5), "lusts" (Rom 1:24), and "suffers" (2 Cor 2:4). It doubts and believes (Rom 10:6–10), is hardened (2 Cor 3:14), and is impenitent (Rom 2:5), but it can be strengthened (1 Thes 3:13; Gal 4:6; 2 Cor 1:22). It is the heart of man that "wills" (Gal 4:9; 1 Cor 4:21; 10:27; etc.).

All these aspects of man's existence are summed up in his "life" (*zōē*), which is itself a God-given gift and expresses the concrete existence of man as he is the subject of his own actions. But the life of man before Christ is one lived "according to the flesh" (Rom 8:12; cf. Gal 2:20). With all his capacities for the conscious, intelligent, and purposeful planning of his life, man without Christ remains one who has not been able to achieve the goal proposed for him. Of his situation Paul can only say, "All men sinned and fall short of the glory of God" (Rom 3:23). Their falling short implies that a destiny of glory was somehow intended for them (cf. Rom 8:18–23). Our sketch of the condition of man before Christ has at times necessarily indicated the difference that Christ made in his existence. A fuller description of that difference now follows in terms of man in Christ.

(Kümmel, W. G., *Man in the NT* [rev. ed.; London, 1963] 38–71. Mehl-Koehnlein, H., *L'homme selon l'Apôtre Paul* [Neuchâtel, 1951]. Robinson, J. A. T., *The Body: A Study in Pauline Theology* [SBT 5; London, 1952] 17–33. Stacey, D., *The Pauline View of Man* [London, 1956].)

(VI) Man in Christ. Christian reconciliation brought about a new union of man with God. Paul calls it a "new creation" (Gal 6:15; 2 Cor 5:17) because it introduced a new mode of existence into man's world, in which Christ and the Christian enjoy, as it were,

a symbiosis. Man shares in this new Christian existence through
faith and baptism, which incorporate him into Christ and the
Church; this incorporation finds a distinctive consummation in the
Eucharist. To these elements of Paul's theology, we now turn.

(A) Faith. The experience whereby man appropriates to
himself the effects of the Christ-event is for Paul faith (*pistis*). This
experience begins with the hearing of the "word" about Christ and
ends in a personal commitment of the whole man to his person and
revelation. It begins as *akoē* (hearing) and ends as *hypakoē* (obedience, submission; cf. Rom 10:17; 1:5; 16:26). Man must open himself to the "word" (*logos*, 1 Cor 15:2; cf. 1:18) or the "message"
(*rēma*, Rom 10:17) that is proclaimed to him. His response must in-
volve the whole man: "If with your lips you acknowledge that Jesus
is the Lord and with your mind you believe that God raised him
from the dead, you will be saved" (Rom 10:9). The faith that man
is asked to put in God or Christ (1 Thes 4:14; 1 Cor 1:21–23; Rom
4:24) is not merely an intellectual assent to some proposition but a
vital, personal commitment engaging the whole man to Christ in all
his relations with God, with other men, and with the world. It is an
awareness of the difference that Christ and his salvific role as *Kyrios*
make in man's history. This underlies the statement of Paul, when
he says, "Now even the physical life I am living I live through faith
in the Son of God who loved me and gave himself for me" (Gal
2:20). Faith as an obedient dedication to God's call in Christ far
transcends the OT idea of fidelity. As *hypakoē*, it is the full acceptance of Christian commitment (2 Thes 1:8; Rom 6:16–17; 16:19), to
the exclusion of reliance on self. The basis of the Christian experience is a new union with God in Christ, an ontological reality that is
not immediately perceived by man's conscious faculties. The lively
commitment of faith must so influence his conscious conduct as to
integrate his psychological activity with the ontological reality
within him. This is integrated Christian living (cf. Gal 2:20; 2 Cor
10:5).

The faith of the Christian is a gift of God just as the whole
salvific process is. "It is by his [Christ's] favor that you have been
saved through faith; and this does not come from you; it is the gift
of God" (Eph 2:8). This is the underlying thought in the whole
discussion of Abraham's faith (Rom 4). Since God accosts a man
as a responsible person, he is free to accept or reject that gracious

call. And faith is but the acceptance or the response on the part of man who realizes that the whole initiative rests with God. The man who does not respond is disobedient and under the power of "the god of this age" (2 Cor 4:4; cf. Phil 1:27; 1 Cor 9:26–27; Eph 2:2). Paul implies by this assertion that disbelief is itself a sin.

In the polemical contexts in which Paul rejects the "deeds of the Law" as a means to justification, he insists that this justification comes through faith (Gal 2:16; cf. Rom 2:20, 28; Phil 3:9). However, his full sense of faith demands that the Christian manifest in his conduct his basic commitment to Christ through deeds of love. "In union with Christ Jesus neither circumcision nor the lack of it means anything, but only faith acting through love" (Gal 5:6). This is why Paul continually exhorts his Christian converts to the practice of all sorts of good deeds. Christian faith is a call to freedom (from the Law, from Sin, from the *sarx*-self), but also a call to a service of love to be shown to other men (Gal 5:13). In this way, faith for Paul is no mere intellectual assent to a proposition of monotheism (cf. Jas 2:14–26). For Paul knows that such service is not accomplished without the activity of God in man: "It is God who in his good will is at work in your hearts, inspiring each decision and action" (Phil 2:13).

(Bultmann, R. and A. Weiser, *Faith* [BKW 10; London, 1961]. Hatch, W. H. P., *The Pauline Idea of Faith* [HTS 2; Cambridge, 1917]. Kuss, O., "Der Glaube nach den paulinischen Hauptbriefen," *TG1* 46 [1956] 1–26. Metzger, B. M., *IPLAP* 149–50. Schlatter, A., *Der Glaube im NT* [5th ed.; Stuttgart, 1963]. Vallotton, P., *Le Christ et la foi: Étude de théologie biblique* [Geneva, 1960] 41–144.)

(B) Baptism. Paul's stress on the role of faith in man's share in the Christ-event is adequately understood only when it is linked to his teaching about baptism. This initiatory rite, which incorporates man in Christ and the Church, was inherited by him from the early Church, as the formulaic expressions that he uses with regard to it make clear. But it is Paul who teaches the early Church the real significance of this rite. The confessional formulas he uses (Rom 10:9; 1 Cor 12:3) may well echo primitive baptismal creeds, but it is Paul who teaches that the condition of Christians as "sons of God through faith" is due to their baptism "into Christ" (Gal 3:26–27). He alludes to a rite, in speaking of a "washing of water" and a "word" (= formula?) in Eph 5:26; but Christians so washed have been "consecrated and made upright" (1 Cor 6:11). They have "put on Christ" as if they were putting on new garments—an allusion to robes worn during the baptismal ceremony? This description of the effects of baptism may seem extrinsic, but it at least expresses the dispositions of Christ, which the baptized person is expected to adopt.

Much more important is Paul's teaching about the identification of the Christian through baptism with the death, burial, and resurrection of Christ. The early Church recorded a recollection of Christ, who had described his own death as a baptism (Mk 10:38; Lk 12:50). But Paul's view of the effects of the Christ-event on believers led him to identify Christians, as it were, with the very salvific phases themselves of Christ's existence. Because "one died for all, therefore all died" (2 Cor 5:14). Prima facie, this seems like an assertion of the vicarious nature of Christ's death, but it must be read in the light of such a passage as the following: "Through baptism we have been buried with him in death, so that just as he was raised from the dead through the Father's glory, we too may live a new life. For if we have grown into union with him by undergoing a death like his, of course we shall do so by being raised to life like him" (Rom 6:4–5). Paul's comparison of baptism with the death, burial, and resurrection of Jesus is often thought to allude to the rite of immersion. Though this mode of baptism may be difficult to establish for the 1st cent. AD, Paul's symbolism is sufficiently preserved if the baptized person was somehow under the water. So identified with Christ in his death, the Christian dies to the Law and to Sin (Gal 2:19; Rom 6:6, 10). Identified with Christ in his resurrection, he shares a new life and the very vitality of the Risen Christ and his Spirit (1 Cor 6:17; Col 2:12–13). The Christian "has grown together" with Christ through this likeness of his death, burial, and resurrection (Rom 6:5). The Christian dies in baptism, and a new man is born (cf. Eph 2:15); he is a "new creation" (Gal 6:15; 2 Cor 5:17). It is the beginning of a new "heavenly" existence with Christ: "Though we were dead because of our offenses God has made us live again with Christ. It is by his grace that we are saved. And he has raised us up with Christ Jesus and made us sit down with him in the heavenly realm" (Eph 2:5–6).

This is no mere individualistic experience for Christians, but a corporate one, for through baptism a special union with all Christians is formed. "For we have all—Jews or Greeks, slaves or free men—been baptized in one spirit to form one body" (1 Cor 12:13; cf. Gal 3:28; Eph 2:15). Man attains salvation, therefore, by identification with a salvific community (*Heilsgemeinde*)—by incorporation into the "body of Christ." This is why Paul compares baptism to Israel's passage through the waters of the Reed Sea (1 Cor 10:1–2). In the waters of baptism the new "Israel of God" (Gal 6:16) is formed.

Paul never quotes a primitive baptismal formula (like Mt 28:19), and yet he apparently echoes an early Trinitarian theologoumenon on baptism: "You have been washed, consecrated, and made upright in the name of the Lord Jesus Christ and in the Spirit of our God" (1 Cor 6:11). The baptized Christian is the "temple of the holy Spirit" (1 Cor 6:19) and an adopted son of the Father in virtue of the Spirit communicated to him (Gal 4:6; Rom 8:9, 14–17). The Spirit so received is the constitutive principle of filial adoption and the dynamic source of Christian life and conduct. "All who are guided by God's Spirit are God's sons" (Rom 8:14). Such passages are the basis of the later theological teaching of the relation of the baptized Christian to the persons of the Trinity.

Only indirectly does Paul use the baptismal formula, "in the name of" (*eis to onoma tou* . . . , 1 Cor 6:11; 1:13, 15). Though it expresses proprietorship and suggests that the baptized person becomes the property of Christ (recall "redemptive acquisition"), Paul prefers to speak of the person as baptized "into Christ" (Rom 6:3; Gal 3:27), sacramentally plunged into Christ himself (see page 68).

(Beasley-Murray, G. R., *Baptism in the NT* [London, 1962]. Delling, G., *Die Zueignung des Heils in der Taufe* [Berlin, 1961]. Fascher, E., "Zur Taufe des Paulus," *TLZ* 80 [1955] 643–48. Flemington, W. F., *The NT Doctrine of Baptism* [London, 1948]. Grail, A., "Le baptême dans l'Epître aux Galates," *RB* 58 [1951] 503–20. Iacono, V., "Il battesimo in S. Paolo," *RBiblt* 3 [1955] 348–62. Schnackenburg, R., *Baptism in the Thought of St. Paul* [tr. G. R. Beasley-Murray; N.Y., 1964]. Tremel, Y. B., "Le baptême, incorporation du Chrétien au Christ," *LumVi* 27 [1956] 81–102. Wagner, G., *Das religionsgeschichtliche Problem von Römer 6, 1–11* [AbhTANT 39; Zürich, 1962].)

(C) Incorporation into Christ. To appreciate the effects of faith and baptism as seen by Paul, we must now turn to his ideas on the incorporation of Christians into Christ. This intimate union of

Christ and Christians is expressed by pregnant prepositional phrases
and also by the use of the figure of the "body of Christ."

(a) PREPOSITIONAL PHRASES. Paul uses chiefly four prepositions with "Christ" as their object to suggest different facets of
Christ's influence on the life of the Christian. The use of each of
them is varied and is often rich with nuances. We can only indicate
here some of the most important implications. The four prepositions
are *dia, eis, syn,* and *en.*

The prep. *dia,* "through," normally expresses the mediation of
Christ in a statement of which the subject is the Father. It may denote his mediation through some activity of his earthly ministry (1
Thes 5:9), of his present state as *Kyrios* (Rom 1:5), or of his eschatological role (1 Thes 4:14). It is the phrase that opens up, as it
were, the path that leads to the Christian's experience *en Christō,*
and eventually *syn Christō.*

The prep. *eis,* "into," especially in the phrase *eis Christon,* has
sometimes been understood as an abridgment of *eis to onoma Christou,* "into the name of Christ." With the vb. *baptizō* this is a possible meaning (see page 67). But *eis Christon* is also used with
pisteuō (believe). In fact, it is mainly found in these two contexts:
belief or baptism in Christ. Actually, it is a pregnant phrase expressing the movement toward Christ that these initial Christian experiences imply. It is the beginning of the Christian's condition *en
Christō* (cf. 1 Cor 10:2). Torn from his original condition ("in
Adam," (1 Cor 15:22), from his natural inclinations ("in the flesh,"
Rom 7:5), and from his ethnic background ("under the Law," 1
Cor 9:20), the believer is solemnly introduced "into Christ" in faith
and baptism. *Eis Christon* denotes, then, the movement of incorporation.

The prep. *syn,* "with," is used not only with the object "Christ"
but is also compounded with verbs and adjectives and can in these
constructions express a double relationship of the Christian to Christ.
Either it suggests the identification of the Christian with the pre-
eminently redemptive acts of Christ's historical and risen life (from
the Passion on), or else it denotes the association of the Christian
with Christ in eschatological glory. In the first case, the identification
is seen above all in the compounds of *syn-.* Aside from some generic
expressions like *symmorphos* (formed with him) or *symphytos*
(grown together with him), these words refer to some phase of

Christ's existence from his passion and death on: *sympaschein* (suffer with), *systaurousthai* (be crucified with), *synapothnêskein* (die with), *synthaptesthai* (be buried with), *synegeirein* (raise with), *syndoxazesthai* (be glorified with), *symbasileuein* (rule with), etc. By contrast, the Christian is never said to be born with Christ, to be baptized with Christ, to be tempted with Christ, etc. These events of the life of Christ were not significant for Paul's soteriology. On the other hand, the phrase *syn Christō* can express the association of the Christian with Christ in eschatological glory; it is his destiny to "be with Christ." See 1 Thes 4:14 (significantly *syn Kyriō*); Rom 6:8; 8:32; 2 Cor 4:14. *Syn*, therefore, pregnantly refers to the two poles of the Christian experience: Identified with Christ at its beginning, the Christian is to be associated with him at its end. In the meantime he is *en Christō*.

Lastly, the prep. *en*, "in," with the object "Christ" occurs 165 times in Paul's letters (including *en Kyriō*, *en autō*). Since the studies of A. Deissmann, the preposition has often been interpreted in a local, spatial sense, and *Christos* has been understood mystically of the glorified Lord identified with the Spirit as some spiritual atmosphere in which Christians are bathed. This is supposed to be Paul's mysticism. But subsequent studies by E. Lohmeyer, A. Schweitzer, F. Büchsel, *et al.*, have brought out other aspects of the phrase (metaphysical, eschatological, dynamic, etc.). A detailed summary is impossible here, but several important distinctions should be made to aid the understanding of this important Pauline phrase. *First,* with the object *Kyrios* the phrase usually occurs in greetings, blessings, exhortations (often with imperatives), and formulations of Pauline apostolic plans and activity. The title *Kyrios* denotes, then, the influence of the Risen Jesus in practical and ethical areas of Christian conduct. *En Kyriō* is hardly ever used of Jesus' historical, earthly activity or of his coming eschatological function. It implies, rather, his present, sovereign intervention and dominion in the life of the Christian. Paul tells the Christian to become "in the Lord" what he really is "in Christ." *Second,* with the object *Christos* the phrase frequently has an instrumental sense, when it refers to the historical, earthly activity of Jesus (Rom 3:24; 2 Cor 5:19; Gal 2:17; Col 1:14; Eph 2:10; etc.). In this sense it is often close to *dia Christou.*

Third, the most common use of the phrase *en Christō* is to express the close union of Christ and the Christian, an inclusion or incorporation that connotes a symbiosis of the two. "If any man is in Christ, he is a new creature" (2 Cor 5:17). This vital union can also be expressed as "Christ in me" (Gal 2:20; 2 Cor 13:5; Rom 8:10; Col 1:27; Eph 3:17). The result is that one belongs to Christ (2 Cor 10:7) or is "of Christ"—a "mystical genitive" that often expresses the same idea (cf. Phlm 1 and Eph 4:1; 3:1; or Rom 16:16 and 1 Thes 1:1). The phrase should not be limited to a spatial dimension, for it often connotes a dynamic influence of Christ on the Christian who is incorporated into him. There are also at times ecclesial (Eph 1:10; Gal 1:22) and even eschatological dimensions to the phrase (Eph 2:6). The Christian so incorporated is actually a member of the body of Christ; he is part of the Whole Christ. Needless to say, there are often times when one hesitates about the precise nuance intended (is it instrumental? inclusive?). Both may be intended, and this is why these phrases are often pregnant with meaning.

(Bouttier, M., *En Christ* [Paris, 1962]. Büchsel, F., " 'In Christus' bei Paulus," ZNW 42 [1949] 141–58. Deissmann, A., *Die neutestamentliche Formel 'in Christo Jesu'* [Marburg, 1892]. Dupont, J., *Syn Christô: L'union avec le Christ suivant Saint Paul* [vol. 1; Bruges, 1952]. Kuss, O., *Der Römerbrief* [Regensburg, 1957–59] 319–81. Neugebauer, F., *In Christus* [Göttingen, 1961]. Nielson, J. B., *In Christ* [Kansas City, 1960]. Wikenhauser, A., *Pauline Mysticism* [N.Y., 1960].)

(b) BODY OF CHRIST. The most typically Pauline figure expressing the corporate identity of Christians with Christ is "the body of Christ." Absent from his early letters (1 Thes, 2 Thes, Gal, Phil), it appears first in 1 Cor, in the letter where Paul copes with divisive Corinthian factions. Christ is not divided, he tells them, formulating a teaching on the unity of all Christians in Christ. The symbol of it is the unity of the body with its members. The figure may be derived from contemporary Hellenistic notions about the state as the body politic; but whatever its origins (see J. A. T. Robinson, *The Body* [London, 1952] 55–58), it certainly denotes more than the idea of the body politic transferred to Christian society. In this philosophical notion, the moral union of citizens conspiring to achieve the common good of peace and well-being is suggested. In 1 Cor 12:12–27 the figure as used by Paul scarcely transcends this idea of moral union of all the members. The spiritual gifts enjoyed by the Corinthians (prophecy, tongues, faith, wisdom, etc.) are to be used for the good of the community, not for its disruption. As all the members and limbs conspire for the good of the body, so it is with the body of Christ, and similarly it is used in the hortatory context of Rom 12:4–5. But more is suggested in 1 Cor 6:15. Paul, warning against the defilement of man's body by sexual license, argues, "Don't you know that your bodies are parts of Christ's body? Am I then to take away from Christ parts of his body and make them parts of a prostitute's? Never! Don't you know that a man who has to do with a prostitute makes one body with her? For 'the two,' says Scripture, 'shall become one flesh.'" The union suggested here is certainly more than moral. Paul's meaning is unmistakable: Somehow Christ and the Christian share a union that implies "one flesh." Recall what was said above (see page 61) about the meaning of *sōma* and *sarx* as designations, not of the physical body as something distinct from the soul, but as the equivalents of the whole, individual person. Paul is not referring to members of a society, but to members of Christ as a physical individual; their union is not so much corporate as corporal. The same conclusion is derived from 1 Cor 10:16–17, where Paul insists on the union of all Christians, which is brought about by their share in the eucharistic bread and cup: "Because there is one loaf, we, many as we are, are one body, for we all share the one loaf." The unity of all Christians is derived from their physical consumption of the one loaf; a oneness is suggested that transcends any mere extrinsic union effected by collaboration to attain a common goal. The figure of marriage in Eph 5:22–33 also points to the same transcendent union.

And yet the Christian and Christ are not physically united like the yolk and albumen of an egg. This is the reason why theologians have often called the union "mystical" (even though Paul does not use the word). The ontological reality that is the basis of the union is the possession of the Spirit of Christ: "We have all been baptized in one Spirit to form one body" (1 Cor 12:13). (Cf. Rom 8:9–11.) This possession of the Spirit springs from the sacramental incorporation of Christians into the body of Christ and is, as it were, the term of Paul's soteriological Christology. From another viewpoint, it has often been called the key to his whole thought.

However, neither in 1 Cor nor in Rom does Paul speak explicitly of the Church as the Body of Christ. The closest one comes to this identification is in 1 Cor 12:27–28, where the formulation is not as developed as it is in his later writings. These two themes—of the Church and of the Body—are independent developments in the Pauline letters, which merge only in the Captivity Letters. In the latter, when the cosmic significance of Christ has clearly dawned upon him, Paul links for the first time the themes of "body," "head," and "church." The Church is then explicitly identified with the "Body of Christ" in formulations that are almost convertible: "He [Christ] is the head of the body, the Church" (Col 1:18; cf. 1:24); God "made him the supreme head of the Church, which is his body" (Eph 1:23). In Eph especially there is great emphasis on the unity of the Church: Christ has broken down the barrier between Jew and Greek; all now share one salvation, for he has "reconciled both sides in one body to God through the cross" (Eph 2:16). "There is only one body and one Spirit, just as there is only one hope in the calling you have received: one Lord, one faith, one baptism, one God and Father of all" (Eph 4:4). And yet with all this stress on the unity of the body and the oneness of all Christians in Christ, Paul never came to speak of "one Church" (*mia ekklēsia*). Is this just fortuitous? Part of the answer appears below in the discussion of "Church." In the Pastoral Letters, otherwise so preoccupied with Church interests, the "Body of Christ" makes no appearance.

Intimately related to the body theme in Paul's letters is the head theme. In the Captivity Letters we learn that Christ is "the head of the body, the Church" (Col 1:18; cf. Eph 1:23). It may seem that this theme is simply an extension of the body theme. But it is not accurate to think that Paul, having portrayed the union of Christ and Christians by the analogy of the body, later concluded that Christ must be its head because the head is the most important part of the body (as can be illustrated in contemporary Hellenistic medical writers; see P. Benoit, *RB* 63 [1956] 27). For the head theme appears early in Paul's letters independently of the body theme, not as a figure of unity, but of subordination. In 1 Cor 11:3ff. Paul argues that women should wear head-coverings in liturgical assemblies because, among other reasons, the order of creation in Gn indicates the subordination of wife to husband. The head covering is the sign of this subordination. Paul concludes, "Christ is the head of every man, while a woman's head is her husband, and Christ's head is God." Paul plays here on the two senses of "head" (the physical head which must be covered, and the figurative head [like "head" of a department]). But there is no mention of body here at all. There is a remnant of this figure of subordination in Col 2:10, where Christ is declared the "head of every principality and power." But in the Captivity Letters the body theme and the head theme are joined: Christ is the head of the body, the Church. The image is exploited, with details from contemporary medical teaching: "Let us rather hold to the truth in charity; thus we shall fully grow up into union with him who is head, Christ. For in dependence on him the whole body is bonded and knit together" (Eph 4:16). This aspect of the subordination of the Christian to Christ the head also underlies the comparison of Christian marriage with the Church: "Just as the Church is in subjection to Christ, so too should wives be subject to their husbands in everything" (Eph 5:24).

The Christian experience, then, which is rooted in the historical reality of the bodily Christ, is a living, dynamic union with the individual *risen body* of the *Kyrios*. The corporate union of all Christians must grow to fill out the total Christ (Eph 1:23); this is the *plērōma* of the cosmic Christ. In the lives of individual Christians this means apostolic suffering that fills up what was lacking in Christ's tribulations on behalf of the Church (Col 1:24). It does not mean that such apostolic suffering adds anything to the strictly redemptive value of the Cross, but that such suffering on behalf of the Church continues in time, that which Christ began, but could not finish in time. It must continue until the cosmic dimensions of the Church are achieved.

(Benoit, P., "Corps, tête et plérôme dans les Épîtres de la Captivité," *RB* 63 [1956] 5–44; *Exégèse et théologie*, 2, 107–53. Best, E., *One Body in Christ* [London, 1955]. Hegermann, H., "Zur Ableitung der Leib-Christi-Vorstellung," *TLZ* 85 [1960] 839–42. Martelet, G., "Le mystère du corps et de l'esprit dans le Christ ressuscité et dans l'église," *VerbC* 12 [1958] 31–53. Percy, E., *Der Leib Christi* [Lund, 1942]. Robinson, J. A. T., *The Body* [SBT 5; London, 1955] 49–83. Thornton, L. S., *The Common Life in the Body of Christ* [2nd ed.; Westminster, 1944]. Wikenhauser, A., *Die Kirche als der mystische Leib Christi nach dem Apostel Paulus* [2nd ed.; Münster, 1940].)

(D) **Eucharist.** In explaining the intimate union of Christ with Christians, Paul uses "the body of Christ" in another sense, viz., to mean his Eucharistic body. "Many as we are, we are one body, for we all share in the one loaf" (1 Cor 10:16). In the Eucharist he finds a source not only of the union of Christians with Christ but also of Christians among themselves.

The earliest account of the institution of the Eucharist in the NT occurs in 1 Cor 11:23–25. Though it is related in origin to the Lucan account (22:15–20) and differs somewhat from that of Mk (14:22–25) and Mt (26:26–29), it is an independent record of the institution, probably derived from the Antiochene church. Paul passes it on as tradition, but his account is not so much an eyewitness report as a quotation from a liturgical recitation of what the "Lord" did at the Last Supper, even with its rubrics ("Do this in memory of me," 11:24). Paul does not recount the event in and for itself, but only alludes to it in discussing other problems. He mentions this sacramental meal as part of his critique of the abuses that had crept into the Corinthian community suppers associated with the Eucharist (1 Cor 11) or in the course of his remarks on the eating of meat sacrificed to idols (1 Cor 10).

For Paul the Eucharist is above all the "Lord's Supper" (*kyriakon deipnon*, 1 Cor 11:20), the repast at which the new people of God eats its "spiritual food" and drinks its "spiritual drink" (1 Cor 10:3–4). In this act it manifests itself as the community of the "new covenant" (11:25; cf. Jer 31:31; Ex 24:8), as it "shares in the table of the Lord" (1 Cor 10:21; cf. Mal 1:7,12). The communion of this people implies its union with Christ and with one another; it is a "sharing [*koinōnia*] in the body of Christ" (10:16).

Three aspects in particular reveal the Eucharist as the source of Christian unity. *First*, it is the ritual and sacramental act whereby Christ's presence with his people is concretized. Paul quotes, in effect, the rite of the liturgical celebration and comments on its meaning in the immediate context (1 Cor 11:27–32): Christ's body and blood are identified with the bread and wine so consumed by the Christian community. Any "unworthy" sharing in that repast would bring judgment on the Christian, for he would be "profaning the body and blood of the Lord" (11:27). Since the Lord is identified with such food, those who partake of it may not violate its sacred character and his presence by abuses of individualism, of disregard of the poor, or of idol-worship. One cannot argue away the realism of the identity of Christ with this Eucharistic food in Paul's teaching, even if Paul does not explain how this identity is achieved. But through this presence the unity of Christians is effected. Thus it is the Eucharistic Christ who alone *brings about* the unity of men in Paul's view.

Second, as a memorial and proclamation of Christ's sacrificial death, it is a rallying point. "As often as you eat this bread and drink of this cup, you proclaim the death of the Lord, until he comes" (1 Cor 11:26). This is why the Christian community is to "do this in memory of" him (11:24). The repetition of this liturgical act in which the Lord's body and blood are made present to nourish his people is a solemn "proclamation" of the salvation event itself. For it is the "death of the Lord"—"for you." It announces once again that saving death to those who partake of the sacramental meal. The sacrificial aspect of that death is brought out by the reference to covenant blood in 11:25; the Eucharistic cup is the blood of the "new covenant" (Jer 31:31), an allusion to the pact replacing the covenant sealed by blood and sacrifice in Ex 24:8. This allusion thus invests the shedding of Christ's blood with an efficacy analogous to that of the sacrifice sealing the covenant of Sinai (cf. also 1 Cor 10:14–21).

Third, there is an eschatological aspect to the Eucharist, for the proclamation of that death must continue "until he comes." It is only Christ in his risen, glorious body who fully accomplishes the salvation of those who partake of the table of the *Kyrios.*

(Boismard, M.-E., "The Eucharist According to Saint Paul," *The Eucharist in the New Testament: A Symposium* [ed. J. Delorme; Baltimore, 1964] 125–39. Neuenzeit, P., *Das Herrenmahl* [StANT 1; Munich, 1960].)

(VII) The Church. For all its rarity in the Gospels (Mt 16:18; 18:17), the word *ekklēsia* is found abundantly in the Pauline letters. It does not occur in the first four chapters of Acts, and thereafter it occurs only once (5:11) in the sense of "church" before the story of Paul begins (8:1, 3). It apparently took some time before the early Christians realized their union in Christ in terms of *ekklēsia.* The abundant data in the Pauline letters do not really contradict this. Incidentally, it should be recalled that even in the three accounts of Paul's conversion in Acts, where the heavenly voice says, "Saul, Saul, why do you persecute me? I am Jesus whom you are persecuting" (9:4–5; 22:7–8; 26:14–15), the Church is never explicitly mentioned. Luke records that Paul had been persecuting the "Lord's disciples" (9:1), the "Way" (22:4), or the "name of Jesus of Nazareth" (26:9, 10). Consequently, we should not include as an element of the revelation on the road to Damascus an explicit awareness of the *Church* as the Body of Christ.

The data in the Pauline letters reveal a similar situation. Paul uses *ekklēsia* in 1–2 Thes (the *Early Letters*) in two senses: either to designate a local church (1 Thes 1:1; 2 Thes 1:1), or in the sense expressed by the phrase, "church of God" (1 Thes 2:14; 2 Thes 1:4). In other words, it either denotes the local congregation of believers dwelling in Thessalonica—a unity developed from their community in belief and worship—or it is a title of predilection for Judean communities (cf. 1 Thes 2:14). It is well known that *ekklēsia* is used in the LXX to translate the Hebr *qāhāl*, the term given to the assembly of the Israelites, particularly in their desert wanderings. They are called the "*ekklēsia* of the Lord" (Dt 23:2) or the "*ekklēsia* of the people of God" (Jgs 20:2; cf. Acts 7:38). But it also refers to the Israelites in liturgical gatherings (1 Kgs 8:55; 1 Chr 29:10). However, Paul's expression, *ekklēsia tou theou*, is unique (except possibly for Neh 13:1 [where ms. S reads *kyriou* against the others] and the Hebr equivalent in the War Scroll [1QM 4:10]). But given the OT background, it was more than likely the apt designation for the primitive local churches in Judea, the first units formed in Christian history and peculiarly linked through their Jewish roots to the Israelite "congregation" of old.

When we move to the *Great Letters,* we find the same two senses again. Here *ekklēsia* refers to the local churches of Galatia, Judea, Macedonia, and Cenchreae (Gal 1:2, 22; 2 Cor 8:1; Rom 16:1). But the title "church of God," though referred to Judean churches (1 Cor 11:16), is now also applied to the church of Corinth. According to L. Cerfaux (*The Church*, 113), this title does not designate the universal Church as manifested at Corinth, but is a Pauline way of flattering a church with which he has had rather stormy relations. He accords to Corinth the title otherwise reserved for the mother churches of Palestine (1 Cor 1:2; 2 Cor 1:1; possibly also 1 Cor 10:32). But in this very extension there is a broadening of Paul's understanding of the idea of *ekklēsia*. It begins to transcend the local barriers. This is the seed of Paul's teaching on the universality of the Church. And it is precisely in 1 Cor that this seed of universality is first found. Paul warns the Corinthians against submitting ordinary matters for settlement to the judgment of men "who are nothing in the Church" (1 Cor 6:4). In 1 Cor 14:5, 12 he speaks

of "doing the Church some good." These could be references to the
local community, but one senses in the use of the word a more general meaning (cf. 1 Cor 12:28).

It is strange that in Rom, the letter so often regarded as the
most representative of Paul's thought, the word *ekklēsia* is absent.
All the occurrences of *ekklēsia* in Rom 16 denote local communities;
but this chapter is most likely not an integral part of Rom.

When we come to the *Captivity Letters* the notion of *ekklēsia*
plays a very important role. It is a crucial part of the "mystery of
Christ," and in it the barrier between Jew and Greek is broken
down; all men are reconciled to God in the one body that is the
Church. In Paul's cosmic view of Christ he is now the head of the
Church, which is his body, and is thereby the head of all creation.
God "has put all things under his feet and made him the supreme
head of the Church, which is his body, the fullness of him who is
filled out, all in all" (Eph 1:22–23). The Church is thus equated
with the fullness of Christ and is given cosmic dimensions that em-
brace all creation. Even the spirits (the principalities and powers)
are to learn about the Father's plan of salvation through it (Eph
3:9–11). Paul praises the Father for his wisdom "through the Church
and through Christ Jesus" (Eph 3:21).

We can thus detect a certain growth in Paul's awareness of what
"the Church" really means for man. In a sense, it is but the development of his understanding of Christ's role in salvation. Man is
baptized "in one Spirit to form one body" (1 Cor 12:13). The unity
of the Christian community in the Church is Paul's great contribu-
tion to Christian theology—a unity that he derives from the single
purpose of the divine plan of salvation. There is "one Lord, one
faith, one baptism, one God and Father of all, who is above us all,
pervades us all, and is within us all" (Eph 3:5–6). Eventually, Paul
came to look on the "Church of God" as a transcendent unit embracing both Jews and Greeks but somehow different from them (cf. 1
Cor 10:32).

Paul is vaguely aware that in the Church there is a structure im-
posed ultimately by the Lord himself (1 Cor 10:14–22; 11:23ff.
14:2–19 for its cult; 1 Cor 12:28; Phil 1:1 for its ministry). It too has
its rules, which he quotes (1 Cor 11:16).

But the Church is "the Israel of God" (Gal 6:16), "the Jerusalem above" (Gal 4:26), "the temple of the living God" (2 Cor

6:16), and the bride of Christ (Eph 5:22–33). The most dynamic concept of the Church that Paul uses is undoubtedly that of the Body of Christ, but it should not obscure the figure of it as a building or a temple, which he also frequently employs. He often speaks of the Christians' duty to "build up" the Church. (See 1 Thes 5:11; Gal 2:9; 6:10; 1 Cor 3:9–17; 8:1–10; 10:23; 14:2–4, 12, 17, 26; 2 Cor 6:16; 10:8; 12:19; 13:10; Rom 15:20; Col 1:23; 2:7; Eph 2:19–22; 3:17; 4:12–16 [the metaphor is mixed here: "building the body of Christ"].)

(Best, E., *One Body in Christ* [London, 1955]. Cerfaux, L., *The Church in the Theology of St. Paul* [N.Y., 1960]. Gärtner, B., *Temple and Community in Qumran and the New Testament* [Cambridge, 1965]. Goossens, W., *L'église, corps du Christ, d'après Saint Paul* [Paris, 1949]. MacRae, G. W., "Building the House of the Lord," *AER* 140 [1959] 361–76. Minear, P. S., *Images of the Church in the New Testament* [Phila., 1960]. Pfammatter, J., *Die Kirche als Bau* [Rome, 1960]. Schmidt, K. L., *The Church* [BKW 2; London, 1950]. Wikenhauser, A., *Die Kirche als der mystische Leib Christi nach dem Apostel Paulus* [Münster, 1940].)

(VIII) Demands of Christian Living. The baptized Christian has become a "new creature" (Gal 6:15). He lives, but it is really Christ who lives in him (Gal 2:20); into this new ontological mode of existence he must integrate his conscious conduct. The new life he lives is reoriented by the historic achievement of Christ, but it still has to face a scrutiny at the eschatological judgment seat of Christ. Though man is certain of the salvation already effected by Christ, each individual still has to "appear in his true colors before the tribunal of Christ, to be repaid with good or evil for the life he has lived" (2 Cor 5:10). This is but another aspect of Paul's eschatology. Though already transferred to the heavenly realm through a pledge (Eph 1:14; 2:6), the Christian still has to make his way through this world. He still has to be saved "from the present wicked world" (Gal 1:4; cf. 1 Cor 7:26, 29–31). He "must not adopt the customs of this world, but by his attitude of mind be transformed so that he can find out what God's will is—what is good, pleasing, and perfect" (Rom 12:2). The Christian lives, then, a life with a double polarity.

This double polarity that characterizes Christian life is why Paul insists that the Christian activated by the Spirit of God (Rom 8:14) can no longer live a life bound by a merely natural, earthly horizon. He is no longer *psychikos* (see page 62), but is *pneumati-*

kos and must fasten his gaze on the horizons of the Spirit. The Spirit is not of this world, but comes from God (1 Cor 2:11). And whereas the material man (*psychikos*) cannot accept what comes from the Spirit (1 Cor 2:14), the spiritual man (*pneumatikos*) is alive to everything, does not stifle the Spirit nor disregard its whisperings, but tests all things and holds to what is good (1 Thes 5:19–22).

The double polarity of Christian life also explains Christian freedom. Paul exhorts his Galatian converts to stand firm in the freedom for which Christ has freed them (5:1), in the freedom from the Law, but also from Sin, from Death, and especially from Self (Rom 6:7–11, 14; 7:24–8:2). And yet all creation still awaits the "glorious freedom of the children of God" (Rom 8:21). In the meantime, the Christian must live as "the freedman of Christ" (1 Cor 7:22), as one "under the law of Christ" (*ennomos Christou*, 1 Cor 9:21).

In other words, Christian freedom is not an antinomian license; Paul vigorously rejects the idea that man should blatantly sin in order that God may more abundantly show forth his mercy to the sinner (Rom 6:1; cf. 3:5–8). There is the "law of Christ" (Gal 6:2). When it is scrutinized, it is seen to be the "law of love." This is explained in terms of "bearing one another's burdens" (in a context of fraternal correction, Gal 6:2). Even more explicitly, in Rom 13:8–10 Paul repeats the 5th, 6th, 7th, and 8th Commandments of the Decalogue and sums them all up in the saying, "You must love your neighbor as you do yourself"; and he concludes, "So love fully satisfies the Law." This is, of course, the "law of the Spirit" (Rom 8:2). Christ has not simply substituted for the Law of Moses another legal code. The "law of the Spirit" may be a reflection of Jer 31:33, but it is more than likely that Paul has coined the phrase to describe the Spirit's activity in terms of *nomos*, about which he has just been speaking. The Spirit's law of love is the new inner source and guide of the life by which the *pneumatikos* lives; it is the ontic principle of vitality, whence springs the love that must interiorize the Christian's entire ethical conduct.

And yet it is to such *pneumatikoi*—to the sons of God guided by the Spirit (Rom 8:14–15)—that Paul addresses his exhortations to virtuous conduct. Usually the latter part of each of his letters is filled with detailed instructions for the Christian's ethical conduct. We single out only a few characteristics. Form criticism has isolated in his letters the catalogues of virtues and vices that should or should not characterize the Christian way of life (cf. Gal 5:19–23; 1 Cor 5:10–11; 6:9–10; 2 Cor 12:20; Rom 13:13). The eschatological reference in these (possibly pre-Pauline, adapted) catalogues is usually evident: "People who do such things will have no share in the Kingdom of God" (Gal 5:21; cf. Rom 2:5–11; Eph 5:5). These lists can be compared with similar catalogues found both among Gk (esp. Stoic) philosophers and Jewish teachers (e.g., the Essenes: cf. 1QS 4:2–6, 9–11).

(See W. D. Davies, *Paul and Rabbinic Judaism*, 111–46.)

Related to these catalogues are the more specific *Haustafeln* (exhortations addressed to the members of the *familia*); they formulate the duties of husbands and wives, parents and children, and masters and slaves (Col 3:18–4:1; Eph 5:21–6:9 [cf. 1 Tm 2:8–15; Ti 2:1–10; 1 Pt 2:18–3:7]). These exhortations represent the closest that Paul comes to a systematic formulation of social ethics; but they are limited to the domestic society and contain only generalities.

Of particular interest are his instructions on slavery, virginity, and marriage. His underlying principle: "There is no room for 'Jew' and 'Greek'; there is no room for 'slave' and 'freeman'; there is no room for 'male' and 'female'; for in union with Christ Jesus you are all one." (Gal 3:28). Considered from the standpoint of union with Christ, such ethnic and social distinctions are valueless. And yet, Paul never tries to change the existing social conditions in the name of Christian teaching. (We state this merely as a fact.) (Cf. 1 Cor 7:21–22.) He sent the runaway slave Onesimus back to his master Philemon, not with the recommendation that he be manumitted, but that he be received "as more than a slave, as a dear brother" (Phlm 16; cf. Sir 33:31). He counsels slaves to obey their masters in all things (Col 3:22–4:1; Eph 6:5–9) and even goes so far as to recommend that they "think of Christ as the master" for whom they are working (Col 3:24). He does not try to change the external conditions of man's existence, but he does point the way to the Christianization and interiorization of the existing situation.

Regarding virginity, Paul clearly states his own opinion. It is not "a command of the Lord" (1 Cor 7:25), but he thinks that he is as attuned to the Spirit in this matter as anyone else (7:40). He recommends "a good thing" to the unmarried and to widow(er)s; at first his statement is absolute and does not imply a comparison: "It is a good thing for a man not to touch a woman" (1 Cor 7:1; cf. 7:7–8). Two reasons are given for this opinion: First, "in view of the present distress," i.e., because of the impending parousia for which Paul longed (1 Cor 7:26, 29–31; cf. 1 Thes 4:15, 17; Rom 13:11). Second, because the unmarried person can devote his undivided attention to the Lord's cause (*ta tou kyriou*, 7:32–34). Here a comparison between the unmarried and married state is implied, and Paul recommends virginity in view of (apostolic?) service of the Lord. At the end of the long ch. 7 Paul introduces the comparison explicitly in the difficult passage concerning the marrying of one's virgin (daughter, ward, fiancée?): "The man who marries her does what is right, but he who does not does even better" (*kreisson poiēsei*, 7:38). There is little doubt, therefore, that throughout the chapter Paul recommends a celibate life to those who can live it. On the other hand, his statements should not be made out to discourage marriage (cf. 7:38, *kalōs poiei*). He knows that each person has received his own special gift in this matter (7:7).

Most of 1 Cor 7, however, is devoted to instructions about marriage itself. Paul retails the mutual, conjugal obligations of husbands and wives (7:2–6). He insists on "no divorce" as the Lord's command (7:10–11), gives instructions about peaceful mixed marriages (7:12–14), and grants his "Pauline privilege" (7:15–16). What is more important, however, is the view that Paul has of the marriage bond itself as the means of the sanctification and salvation of the spouses (7:14, 16). Even in the case of the mixed marriage he teaches that the believing spouse is the source of a "consecration" of the unbelieving partner and that both of them are the same for their children (7:14). When Paul insists on the subordinate place of the wife in domestic society, he is echoing the contemporary social structure that he knew, in which the woman was far more subject to the man than she is today. Such a view is found in 1 Cor 11:3, 7–12; 14:34–35; 2 Cor 11:3; see the contemporary dim view of women painted in the rabbinical writings (*ThDNT* 1, 777–84).

But it is the same Paul who also wrote Gal 3:28 and the exalted view of marriage in Eph 5:22–33. Christian tradition has adopted from him the view of man as the head of the household, but it has not made capital of his emphasis on the subordinate role of woman. In Eph 5:22–33 he teaches the subordination of the wife to the husband (as in 1 Cor 11:3), but he also clearly tempers it with the instruction to the husband to love his wife, "just as Christ loves the church and gave himself for her" (Eph 5:25). This passage is part of a *Haustafel*, and it is Paul's instruction on Christian marriage, wherein he compares it to the union of Christ and his Church. He sees in the subjection of the wife and the love of the husband a reflection of the intimate union of Christ and his Church. Quoting Gn 2:24, "For this reason a man leaves father and mother and clings to his wife, and the two become one flesh," he reveals a "secret" (*mystērion*) hidden in that verse for long centuries, that the fundamental union of marriage established by God long ago was a prefigured "type" of the union of Christ and his Church. This view of the sublimity of the marriage bond transcends all the regulations that Paul lays down for it in 1 Cor 7.

Paul has instructions for Christian conduct in many other areas, which cannot be discussed in this brief sketch. We conclude our remarks on Paul's ethical teaching in general by insisting on its Christocentrism. As Christ was the "image of God" (1 Cor 11:7; 2 Cor 4:4; Col 1:15), so man in his earthly existence is to be the "image of the heavenly man" (1 Cor 15:49; cf. Rom 8:29). It is growth in Christ that Paul recommends to his readers, contemporary and modern. In this way the Christian lives his life "for God" (Gal 2:19). "You have stripped off your old self with its ways and have put on that new self newly made in the likeness of its Creator, to know him fully" (Col 3:10). Significantly, with all his emphasis on Christ, Paul once again refers the Christian ultimately to the Father—through Christ.

(Allmen, J. J. von, *Pauline Teaching on Marriage* [London, 1963]. Coleman-Norton, P. R., "The Apostle Paul and the Roman Law of Slavery," *Studies in Roman Economic and Social History* [Princeton, 1951]. Delling, G., *Paulus' Stellung zu Frau und Ehe* [BWANT 56; Stuttgart, 1931]. Didier, G., *Désintéressement du Chrétien* [Paris, 1955]. Enslin, M. S., *The Ethics of Paul* [Cambridge, 1930]. Grelot, P., *Man and Wife in Scripture* [N.Y., 1964]. Legrand, L., *The Biblical Doctrine of Virginity* [N.Y., 1963]. Lowrie, W., " 'Glorify God in Your Body,' " *TTod* 10 [1953–54] 492–500. Montague, G.T., *Growth in Christ: A Study in Saint Paul's Theology of Progress* [Kirkwood, Mo., 1961]. Vögtle, A., *Die Tugend- und Lasterkataloge im NT* [NTAbh 16/4–5; Münster, 1936]. Wibbing, S., *Die Tugend- und Lasterkataloge im NT* [Beiheft z. ZNW 25; Berlin, 1959].)

General Bibliography

Amiot, F., *The Key Concepts of St. Paul* (N.Y., 1962). Bonsirven, J., *L'Évangile de Paul* (Paris, 1948); *Exégèse rabbinique et exégèse paulinienne* (Paris, 1929). Bornkamm, G., *Das Ende des Gesetzes: Paulinische Studien* (2nd ed.; Munich, 1958). Bover, J. M., *Teología de San Pablo* (Madrid, 1946). Bultmann, R., *TNT* 1, 185–352. Cerfaux, L., *Christ in the Theology of St. Paul* (N.Y., 1959); *The Church in the Theology of St. Paul* (N.Y., 1959); *Le Chrétien dans la théologie de Saint Paul* (LD 33; Paris, 1962). Cullmann, O., *The Christology of the New Testament* (2nd ed.; Phila., 1963). Dodd, C. H., *The Meaning of Paul for Today* (London, 1920). Feine, P., *Die Theologie des Neuen Testaments* (8th ed.; Berlin, 1953) 145–308. Grossouw, W. K. M., *In Christ* (Westminster, Md., 1952). Klausner, J., *From Jesus to Paul* (London, 1944). Lohmeyer, E., *Grundlagen paulinischer Theologie* (Tübingen, 1929). Lyonnet, S., "Pauline Soteriology," R-F, *INT* 820–65; *De peccato et redemptione* (2 vols.; Rome, 1958–60). Munck, J., *Paul and the Salvation of Mankind* (London, 1959). Purdy, A. C., "Paul the Apostle," *IDB* 3, 681–704. Schoeps, H., *Paul* (London, 1961). Schweitzer, A., *The Mysticism of Paul the Apostle* (London, 1931); *Paul and His Interpreters* (N.Y., 1912). Tondelli, L., *Il pensiero di S. Paolo* (2nd ed.; Turin, 1948). Whiteley, D. E. H., *The Theology of St. Paul* (Oxford, 1964).

    Ellis, E. E., *Paul and His Recent Interpreters* (Grand Rapids, 1961). Metzger, B. M., *IPLAP* 131–62. Rigaux, B., *Saint Paul et ses lettres* (Bruges, 1962). Schnackenburg, R., *Neutestamentliche Theologie* (Munich, 1963) 84–106.

Indexes

Subject Index

Abba, Father, 11
Abraham, 21, 27, 31, 59, 64
Adam, 7, 10, 26, 28, 40, 41, 42, 54, 55, 56, 57, 68
Amen, 11
Analogy of faith, 3
Angels, spirits, 32, 40, 47, 56, 57, 77
Anthropology, 9, 16, 17, 28, 53, 61
Antioch, 8, 13
Apocalyptic, 22, 30, 31
Apostle, 11, 12, 14, 19
Aramaic, 7, 22, 35, 36
Ascension, 13
Asia Minor, 14, 22, 35
Atonement, 44, 46, 47

Baptism, 1, 43, 53, 59, 64-68, 72
Blood, 44, 46, 47, 61, 74, 75
Body, 7, 16, 59, 61, 71, 73
Body of Christ, 59, 67, 68, 70-73
  =Church, 28, 67, 71-73, 76, 77
  =Eucharist, 73-75

Call, 23, 24, 27, 72
Captivity Letters, 4, 14, 21, 40, 72, 73, 77
Catalogues of vices, virtues, 80
Cephas, 13
Christ-event, 4, 17, 18, 28, 30, 49, 50, 51, 52, 53, 64, 66
Christocentrism, 16, 22, 26
Christology, 9, 17, 23, 28, 31, 42, 71
Church, 5, 9, 10, 13, 16, 19, 20, 22, 28, 31, 32, 37, 38, 66, 71-73, 75-78, 82
Circumcision, 65
Command of the Lord, 80
Confessional formulas, 11, 35, 65

Cosmic role of Christ, 14, 22, 25, 26, 28, 77
Covenant, 9, 27, 46, 49, 51, 60, 74, 75
Creation, new, 40, 41, 63, 66, 70, 78
Cross, 10, 16, 38, 44, 47, 72, 73
Curse, 10, 18, 58, 59, 60

Damascus, 8, 9, 10, 11, 13, 15
Death, 16, 29, 40, 49, 50, 54, 55, 56
Death of Jesus, 4, 9, 10, 12, 13, 20, 33, 38, 39, 41, 43, 44, 47, 59, 60, 66, 69, 75, 79
Deeds (works of the Law), 57, 60, 65
Demythologization, 17, 18, 23
Development of dogma, 3, 4, 42
Divorce, 81

Early Letters, 4, 29, 70, 76
Ego, 59, 62
End of the Law, 27, 59
Ephesus, 29
Eschatology, 4, 28, 29, 30, 31, 42, 75, 78, 80
Eschaton, 4, 10, 22, 23, 28, 29, 30, 40
Eucharist, 11, 13, 39, 73-75
Europe, 14
Exegesis, 3
Expiation, 39, 43, 44, 45, 46, 47

Faith, 9, 16, 20, 22, 30, 31, 40, 43, 52, 53, 57, 64-65, 67, 72
Father, 1, 2, 8, 9, 12, 20, 21, 23, 24, 25, 26, 28, 29, 34, 40, 41, 42, 43, 44, 46, 47, 48, 67, 68, 72, 77, **82**
Filial adoption, 27, 43, 57
Flesh, 7, 16, 27, 59, 61-62
Freedom, 17, 26, 37, 48, 49, 50, **59**, 65, 79

84

86

Index of Modern Authors